Cucina Piemontese
COOKING FROM ITALY'S PIEDMONT

Cucina Piemontese

COOKING FROM ITALY'S PIEDMONT

Maria Grazia Asselle & Brian Yarvin

HIPPOCRENE BOOKS
NEW YORK

Jacket and book design by Michael Yee.
Photography by Brian Yarvin.

For more information, address:
HIPPOCRENE BOOKS, INC.
171 Madison Avenue
New York, NY 10016

ISBN 0-7818-1123-6
Cataloging-in-Publication Data available from the Library of Congress.
Printed in the United States of America.

Sommario

[C O N T E N T S]

Maria's great aunt Natalina and her husband Pietro, circa 1912.

Prefazione

[P R E F A C E]

When you're a child, you take everything for granted. At least that was my experience growing up in Torino in the 1960s and '70s. My family had strong ties to Langhe, where my mother's relatives lived and worked on their farms. Every other Sunday we visited them in towns like Dogliani and Carrù, returning to the city loaded down with fresh vegetables, fruit, eggs, and maybe even a rabbit. There could also be *grissette*—the thick soft breadsticks made by local bakers—and the round *tome*, Langhe's most well-known cheese.

We would then visit my father's hometown, Bra, to buy meat, the famous *salsiccia di Bra*, and my mother's favorite candies from a local pastry shop. In season, we might have also stopped along the way for produce from local farmers. My mother especially loved peppers from Carmagnola, which she preserved in oil and vinegar for winter.

When my family spent weekends and vacations in Entracque, a village in the mountains just outside Cuneo, we ate local potatoes, purchased directly from the producers. There in the springtime, we gathered wild spinach and other greens—they were the tastiest I'd ever had—and in the summer, we'd go mushroom hunting and berry picking. In the winter, the preserved mushrooms and jam on the table would remind us of our efforts.

All this seemed normal and was ordinary for families like mine whose older generation had moved to the "big city" but still lived geographically close to their native towns.

Until recently, I thought this was an experience common in all of Italy. A couple of years ago, a friend from Lecco, on Lake Como, drove me from the Malpensa airport to Entracque. The trip was 250 kilometers across

*Natalina, Pietro, and their grown children Rosa, Lino, and Angela
in front of their house in Carru, circa 1960.*

Piemonte from the northeast to the southwest, and largely on two-lane roads. Along the way, and especially when we got to Cuneo, I pointed out what foods the different places offered. At Bra there were sausages, asparagus, tiny pastries, and cheese; meats from the Piedmontese breed of cattle in Carrù; fruit in the Saluzzo countryside; peppers from Carmagnola; and in Cuneo candied chestnuts and chocolate truffles (Cuneesi). In Borgo San Dalmasso there were snails and jams by Agrimontana, and Castelmagno and other cheeses from the mountains. My friend was astonished by the richness of the land and how every corner of it had something special to offer.

The province of Cuneo is at the heart of a food culture deeply rooted in its local products. After many years, through the eyes of my friend, I came to realize how lucky I was to have been exposed to all that goodness in my formative years, when I developed a sense of taste and a passion for food.

For my husband Brian, Piedmontese cooking was initially a shock. When I met him in 1984, one thing that brought us together was our sense of adventure. However, he had grown up in a country where the concern for cholesterol had made people fearful of eating butter, dairy products and meat. During his first visit in 1985 he was surprised to see butter used in all sorts of dishes, even served with slices of salami and ham as an appetizer. The quantity, variety, and quality of the cheeses at my parents' house astonished him just as much. Even more startling to Brian was raw meat salad (page 34) and *salsiccia di Bra*; eventually he came to appreciate them both. In Piemonte, his understanding of Italian food was turned upside down.

Piemonte, located at the western extreme of Italy, has a beautiful, varied landscape. The mountains that surround it isolate its inhabitants physically and psychologically from the rest of the country and few tourists venture to explore it. Piemonte has become better known among food lovers in the last fifteen years thanks to Slow Food, the worldwide organization born in Bra that promotes sustainable agriculture and traditional products. Events such as the February 2006 Winter Olympics have also brought world-wide attention to this area of Italy. People that had never heard of Piemonte before have now read of it, seen it on television, and learned about its foods and traditions. Hopefully, this will inspire them to learn more about this corner of Italy, to explore its beauty, and to savor its food. We would like this book to be your introduction and companion for the journey.

Maria Grazia Asselle
Edison, New Jersey
Augustl 2005

Ringraziamenti

[A C K N O W L E D G M E N T S]

Despite our having cooked and eaten thousands of Piedmontese meals, we could never have written this book alone. We received lots of helpful advice and counsel from Piedmontese food guru Marina Cravero of Turin, Italy. She helped us make sure that our recipes were authentically Piedmontese. Maria's cousin, Francesca Bracco of Dogliani, interviewed some of her town's best cooks on our behalf, gleaning invaluable information.

People here in the United States were no less helpful. The crews at two butcher shops; John's in Scotch Plains, New Jersey and Giovanni Esposito & Sons in Manhattan both went above and beyond the call of duty to explain how American cuts of meat can be adapted to Piedmontese cooking methods.

We also had input from two experts in the field: Marco Buzzio of Salumeria Biellese in Manhattan, one of the most knowledgeable sausage makers there is, and Chef Peter Bernstein of Berta's Chateau in Wanaque, New Jersey, one of the few restaurants to still serve *fonduta*, bollito misto and other classics in an area that was once a Piedmontese stronghold.

We are indebted to our editor, Rebecca Cole of Hippocrene Books; without her help this would just be a jumbled stack of scrap paper.

Finally, this book is dedicated to Maria's late parents, Rosa and Masino. The lessons we both learned from them were a strong beginning.

Lo Stile di Vita Piemontese

[T H E   P I E D M O N T E S E   L I F E S T Y L E]

On any sunny weekend day, the people of Piemonte head outdoors. You'll find them hiking the region's remarkable network of trails, kayaking its world-class whitewater, bicycling winding back roads, rock climbing on great cliffs, and of course skiing in the Alps.

But when lunchtime comes, they don't pull out brown-bagged sandwiches. Instead, they visit small country restaurants and huts high in the mountains where traditional foods are offered: wild mushrooms preserved in oil, polenta served on wooden planks, boiled and stewed meats, and Zuppa Inglese. Alongside will be local wines; not the Barolos and Barbarescos that line the racks of the world's most expensive shops, but Spanna, Dolcetto, Barbera, and other outstanding and affordable selections.

After the meal is finished, one might down a thimbleful of herb-infused grappa (many mountain huts display jugs of grappa in various states of infusion) before returning to the trail. Piemonte is the sort of place one is as likely to visit for kayaking or snowshoeing as for gastronomy. Here, outdoor activities are as important to daily life as good eating.

This isn't the part of Italy where you'll see crowds of people lingering in bars or chatting idly. It is a place where people work hard—Torino is the industrial center of Italy, one of Europe's most important business centers. Fine restaurants just as easily host important business meetings as a groups of gourmets.

Most important, Piemonte is a place where nothing is done as an afterthought. If the region had a slogan, it would be, "Don't do something if you aren't going to do it right." Here, when you go for hike in the mountains, go to a business meeting, or cook a fine meal, it's done with unequaled energy and purposefulness. Nowhere is this more evident than in its great cuisine.

PIEMONTE

Biella•

Novara•

Vercelli•

Torino•

•Asti

•Pinerolo

Bra• •Alba

Barolo•

•Dogliani

Carru•

•Cuneo

Geografia e Storia

[GEOGRAPHY & HISTORY]

For decades, the city of Turin, Italy, and its surrounding area were known more for heavy industry than cuisine, but over the past ten years or so, its food and wine have become recognized as a remarkable culinary bridge between France and Italy. This area is collectively known as "the Piedmont"— Piemonte in Italian—and, as the name implies, it encompasses the foothills of the Alps. In the Middle Ages, it was incorporated within the Duchy of Savoy in western France, which became the Kingdom of Savoy in 1713, with its capital in Turin.

Piedmont is as far west in Italy as you can go, surrounded by mountains on three sides. These barriers are at the root of many Piedmontese traits: its strong ties to local food and wine traditions; the still-active use of dialect; the reserved and conservative character of its people; and its architecture— with its widespread use of covered walkways, known as *portici*, along the main streets of towns and cities—a unique response to its climate, humid with hot summers, foggy autumns, and snowy winters.

Piemonte's wide variety of landscapes influences agricultural production and gives root to the diversity of its food. In addition to mountains, Piedmont comprises large hilly areas (Langhe and Monferrato) and sweeping plain area (Canavese, Vercellese, Novarese, and Lomellina). In the hills, wine growing is the most developed agricultural activity. Among those produced are Barolo and Barbaresco, universally recognized as Italy's greatest red wines. The swampy areas around the cities of Novara and Vercelli have become Europe's largest rice-growing region. Grazing lands in the hills and mountains offer the best conditions for raising cattle, and the areas of Cuneo, Alba, Asti, and Torino are home to a native breed known (naturally) as the "Piemontese." It is lean, tender, and recognized for its excellent flavor. Thanks to the favorable grazing conditions, dairy products play a major role in local cuisine—indeed, eight of the thirty Italian D.O.P.[1] cheeses are made here.

Because of its Alpine position, nearby Mediterranean flavors had little influence on Piedmontese cooks and, without access to seafood, a cuisine dominated by meat and dairy has taken firm hold. The only fish traditionally eaten in Piemonte are preserved anchovies, salt cod (baccalà), and fresh trout—the two salted items having been imported from Spain and Portugal since the Middle Ages, the other plentiful in mountain streams. The Romans brought olive oil, and it partially replaced the use of animal fat in cooking, but butter and lard are still very common. Other characteristics of this cuisine are the consumption of raw vegetables, rice as a staple food, truffles, and the heavy use of garlic.

The Piedmontese table is rich in variety. Meals can begin with an aperitif like Vermouth, progress to hot and cold appetizers such as Vitello Tonnato (page 35), followed by a first course of pasta, rice, or polenta. A second course of meat with vegetables on the side, such as *Brasato al Vino Rosso* (page 90), would follow, and a tray of cheeses and one of the region's creative desserts—perhaps *Bonet*, the chocolate and amaretti flan (page 127), or Zabaione, an egg custard (page 130)—would complete the meal.

In order to describe the world of Piedmontese food completely, we need to look at the various parts of the region. Each has its own personality, shaped by history and environment. Monferrato and Langhe are bordering, hilly areas whose major centers are Asti and Alba. Their cuisines are similar but Langhe is more prestigious due to the presence of great wines: Barolo, Barbaresco, and Nebbiolo. Internationally renowned for their complexity and character, they lend an aristocratic touch to local tables.

Perhaps the most legendary ingredient from Langhe and Monferrato is the truffle, the underground fungus that has long captivated gourmets. Of the two kinds, white and black, white truffles are considered of higher quality

1- *D.O.P. (Protected Designation of Origins) means that the European Community officially recognizes: (1) an agriculture or food product is specific to an area; (2) its quality or characteristics are essentially or exclusively due to a particular geographical environment; and (3) its production, processing, and preparation take place in the defined geographical area.*

because their scent is more intense. They're best used raw and are generally thinly shaved over a dish just before it is eaten.

Langhe's cuisine is only one of several in the province of Cuneo. Cheese is central here, and many, some with ancient origins, are eaten either by themselves or used as an ingredient. A well-known variety is Castelmagno, mentioned in eighteenth-century documents as having been used as a form of payment by the inhabitants of Val Grana. Nowadays it is produced in the towns of Castelmagno, Pradleves, and Monterosso Grana. It is made entirely with milk from the white cows of the Piedmontese breed and aged in caves for two to five months. It's served both as a table cheese and also used in recipes like gnocchi (page 54). Murazzano, named after the town of the same name in Alta Langa, is another classic table cheese whose origin can be traced to the time when Celts lived in the area. It is at least 60 percent sheep's milk. While aging from a minimum of four to a maximum of ten days, its cylindrical forms are washed daily with lukewarm water. When ready, each weighs about ten to fourteen ounces; it is soft, white, compact, and without a crust. Murazzano can be eaten at the end of a meal as is, or dressed with extra-virgin olive oil and freshly ground black pepper.

There's also a huge variety of salami and other sausages. Traditionally, each farming family raised pigs. Various methods of sausage making developed, and one of the most typical varieties is *bale d'aso* (literally "donkey's testicles") from Mondovì, near Cuneo—an almost spherical sausage. Pork skin was traditionally stuffed with donkey meat, but these days a mix of lean and fatty pork and beef seasoned with spices and salt is used instead. It's boiled and served hot with mashed potatoes, lentils or other beans. Also worth mentioning is the fresh veal sausage produced in Bra. In 1867 a royal decree made all veal sausages but the Bra variety illegal. Since then, the art of making it has been transmitted secretly from generation to generation of local butchers. Lean veal mixed with 10 to 30 percent lard is ground and seasoned with salt, pepper, nutmeg, and cinnamon. Sometimes fennel seeds, garlic, white wine, grated Parmesan or *toma delle Langhe* cheese are added. Finally, the mixture is stuffed into pig's intestines. The result is delicate and tasty, whether eaten raw, grilled, used in sauces for pasta, or as a stuffing ingredient.

While veal is the most popular meat in Piedmont, many signature meat dishes use beef. For *Brasato* (page 90), large pieces are braised for hours in robust, local red wines such as Barolo. Bollito Misto (page 94) is another typical dish using several cuts of beef (these can include the head, beef round, oxtail, and tongue) in addition to boiled sausage, and hen or capon. Given the large amount of meat used in preparing it, Bollito Misto is meant to be eaten around the table with family and friends. It's served with different sauces, the most common of which are Bagnet Verd (green sauce) and Bagnet Ross (red sauce) (pages 96-97.)

The rich harvest of corn and wheat also finds its way into the Piedmontese diet. In the mountains, Polenta (page 58) was traditionally a staple, while the towns preferred refined white bread (grissini), and freshly made pasta. Among the latter, Tajarin (page 42) is the best known. Similar to angel's hair pasta, it's the Piedmontese version of egg noodles. The classic version dresses the pasta with sauce made from the juices of roast meat; its apex is reached during the truffle season, when the noodles are boiled, dressed with butter, grated Parmesan cheese, and thin shavings of white truffle.

The refined cuisine of Turin also includes many rice dishes, such as risotto and soups. But the area where rice rules lays north of Turin, around the cities of Biella, Novara, and Vercelli. In fact, their most typical dish is probably a risotto called *Paniscia* (page 62) in Novara and Panissa in Vercelli. Both dishes are based on rice, fresh borlotti beans, butter, and a sausage preserved in fat—*salam d'la duja* (*duja* is the dialectal name of the terra-cotta container the sausage is preserved in). *Paniscia* is further enriched by fresh vegetables and wine, and is traditionally—unlike the Vercelli version—served without grated cheese. Also from Biella is a rice dish called *Riso in Cagnon* (page 61), in which rice is cooked al dente, drained, and mixed with cheese and melted butter.

Piedmontese farmers produce a huge variety of vegetables and fruits, including many less familiar varieties like cardoons. The *cardo gobbo* (hutched cardoon) is considered the best. They're eaten along with other raw vegetables as part of Bagna Cauda (page 26), but they are also served with Besciamella. Peppers are commonly cultivated here as well. Often roasted and served with a dressing of garlic, oil and anchovies as an appetizer, they are also found as Peperonata (page 106), stewed in oil, garlic, onions, and tomato sauce, and sometimes cooked along with rabbit or chicken. Pears and apples grown in the Saluzzo countryside are used to prepare all sorts of cakes and pastries, or cooked with wine and spices (page 132).

Chestnuts and hazelnuts are also used in cakes, pastries and desserts. Chestnuts are commonly eaten roasted or boiled. However, prepared as marrons glacés—large candied chestnuts— they become a classic regional dish created in the sixteenth century at the Savoy court, and popular among nobles and rich families throughout Europe. The production of the chestnuts used to make these sweets today is very limited, and most of their raw source—a special type that has one large and two atrophied fruits in each husk—comes nowadays from the area of Viterbo, northeast of Rome—well outside Piemonte.

Hazelnuts are the main ingredient in *Torta di Nocciole* (page 124), a specialty of bakers in Langhe and Roero, as well as in *Baci di Dama* (page 117), two half-moons of sweet, buttery dough mixed with ground roasted hazelnuts, glued together with melted dark chocolate. Historically, Cuneo's hazelnuts have been exported to other areas of Piedmont and, in 1865, Caffarel—Turin's famous candy maker—used hazelnut flour in the manufacturing of *Gianduiotti*, the chocolate symbol of Turin, to celebrate Carnevale.

It should come as no surprise that the food best symbolizing Turin is made with chocolate. Having been the capital of the Kingdom of Savoy and then the first capital of Italy, this is where rich and noble families made their home and developed a taste for fine dining. Sixteenth-century documents show that the production of chocolate was already important. Initially, wealthy families developed the custom of mixing powdered chocolate as a drink with coffee, milk, and sugar. Then, in the nineteenth century when public cafés became popular, it was offered hot in a glass with a metal handle and called *bicerin* ("little glass"). From chocolate powder used in preparing drinks, developed the art of making solid chocolate. Swiss chocolatiers went there to learn how to handle it. The success of chocolate in Turin is a reminder of how much the Piedmontese people love sweets. Delicacies like *bignole*—miniature pastries filled with a variety of flavored custards and covered with colorful icing—originated in Turin and later spread all over Italy.

In contrast to the cities, the traditional diet in the mountains is centered on few simple products: polenta, potatoes, chestnuts, bread, eggs, cheese. Pasta, rice, and meat appeared only for the holidays. Corn was introduced in Piedmont later than in other areas of Italy. In fact, the first Piedmontese cookbook—*Cuoco Piemontese*—published in 1766, does not mention it even though it was already popular in neighboring Lombardy.

Polenta was sometimes the only source of nutrition for poor peasants who came to suffer from pellagra, a disease caused by a lack of niacin. Because of this link, the cornmeal porridge was almost banned from the table between the end of the nineteenth and the beginning of the twentieth centuries. Fortunately, it survived; knowledge of nutrition and improved economic conditions helped eradicate the disease. Offered on a large wooden serving platter, polenta is a communal dish eaten with cheeses and sauces, topped with sausages and stews made with meats that include boar and venison.

Throughout the centuries, the food and cooking of Piemonte have evolved and spread to other regions, and some of its dishes such as Vitello Tonnato and Panna Cotta have become classics of Italian cuisine. Because of their deep, local roots, however, most of them remain close to home, and close to the hearts of the people who've been making them for all these centuries.

Antipasti

[A P P E T I Z E R S]

Every meal in Piemonte begins with antipasti. These dishes are designed to wake up your appetite and arouse your interest in the food to come. Antipasti are among the most varied dishes at the Piedmontese table. The kaleidoscope of flavors they bring to the table is unparalleled: from anchovies with an olive oil and parsley sauce; and cipolline onions marinated in good vinegar; to rolls of ham in aspic; and *Insalata Russa*, the traditional potato salad. Be they hot or cold; fish, meat, or vegetable, antipasti at the table tells us that there's a real meal ahead. Indeed, it wouldn't be a proper meal without them.

Several Piedmontese antipasti use mayonnaise as a dressing. You can make these recipes with commercial mayonnaise. Adding the juice of one lemon to each cup of mayonnaise, however, will greatly improve its flavor.

Grissini
Breadsticks

No Piedmontese meal is complete without breadsticks. Grissini are almost never made at home in Piemonte and it's their loss; the popular commercial grissini look and taste like dusty chopsticks—indeed that's what Brian's father thought they were when he first saw them—and these homemade ones really stand out.

MAKES 12 BREADSTICKS

1 tablespoon sugar

⅗ ounce yeast

4 cups flour

1 teaspoon salt

In a large bowl, dissolve the sugar in 1 cup of warm water. Add the yeast and let it stand for 10 minutes. Add the flour and the salt to the yeast mixture and knead it into a dough. This will take at least 5 minutes, until the dough is really elastic. Put the dough in a bowl, cover it with a clean dish cloth, and let it stand for 2 hours in a warm place.

Preheat the oven to 375°F and grease a baking sheet. Cut the dough into 12 pieces and stretch and roll them into long sticks. With practice you'll be able to get them really thin, but make sure they are no wider than ⅜ inch. Lay the breadsticks on the prepared baking sheet. Bake for 30 minutes, turning them once or twice to make sure they brown evenly.

They are ready when they are golden brown all over. Serve with any meal—breakfast, lunch, or dinner.

Note: *Grissini* means thin breadsticks, if bigger than ⅜ inch around, they will still be great, they'll just be called *rubatá* instead.

Soma d'Aj
Piedmontese Garlic Bread

4 SERVINGS

1 loaf crusty bread*

4 garlic cloves, halved

3 tablespoons extra-virgin olive oil

1 teaspoon salt

Usually called a "Peasant" loaf or a "Panella."

A poor relative of bruschetta, this is what Maria's grandfather ate for breakfast before heading to the fields. Crushing the garlic by hand will definitely bring you back to those days. Of course, garlic lovers will eat this at every meal, not just with morning coffee. Maria's grandfather ate the cloves of raw garlic after rubbing his bread with them, but this is optional.

In the summer, it's great with fresh tomatoes and, in the fall, with sweet grapes. Except at breakfast, it's accompanied with a glass of good red wine. Don't look for this dish in a Piedmontese restaurant; it's strictly for home and picnic consumption.

Cut the loaf into quarters and toast or grill until golden brown. Vigorously rub each piece of bread with the cut side of a clove of garlic. Drizzle with the olive oil, sprinkle with salt, and serve.

Cipolle Ripiene
Stuffed Onions

This is one of those dishes made from left-overs—and in Piemonte that almost always means a roast.

Preheat the oven to 325°F. Grease a baking sheet with olive oil.

Bring a large pot of water to a boil.

If the sausage isn't already cooked, poke a few holes in the skin and sauté it over medium heat until the skin is well browned and it is cooked through. Set aside.

Add the onions to the boiling water and cook for 5 minutes. Drain and cut off the tops, about one-third from the root end. Spoon out a cavity in the cooked onion. Chop the removed portion and set aside.

Remove the sausage from the casing and combine it with the veal, eggs, parsley, cheese, chopped onion, salt, and pepper.

Fill the hollowed onions with the meat mixture and dot ½ teaspoon of butter on top of each. Place the stuffed onions on the prepared baking sheet and sprinkle the bread crumbs on top. Bake for 1 hour and serve warm.

4 SERVINGS

½ pound sweet Italian sausage or roast pork

4 large onions, peeled

½ pound roast veal (see Arrosto di Vitello, page 93), minced

2 eggs

½ cup chopped fresh Italian parsley

½ cup grated Parmesan cheese

1 teaspoon salt

½ teaspoon freshly ground black pepper

1 tablespoon butter

½ cup dry bread crumbs

Cipolline in Agro Dolce
Sweet-and-Sour Onions

4 SERVINGS

1 pound small onions*

1 cup red wine vinegar

½ cup olive oil

3 tablespoons sugar

½ teaspoon salt

***In Italy, cipolline—small, flat onions—are used; substitute pearl onions if you must.**

These onions show up at almost every meal in Piemonte. Sometimes they're a cold appetizer in their own right, but they can also become an ingredient in other dishes, such as Insalata Russa (page 28).

Bring 4 quarts of water to a boil and blanch the cipolline for 3 minutes. Drain cool, and remove the skins.

In a saucepan, bring the vinegar to a boil and add the oil, sugar, salt, and onions. Lower the heat simmer until the onions are fork tender and the sauce is reduced to a syrupy consistency, about 30 minutes.

Serve hot or cold.

Caponet
Stuffed Zucchini Blossoms

4 SERVINGS

12 zucchini blossoms

½ cup dry bread crumbs

1 cup whole milk

¼ pound ground veal

¼ pound mild Italian sausage

½ teaspoon salt

1 cup chopped fresh parsley

2 cloves garlic

6 sage leaves

1 teaspoon chopped fresh mint

½ cup grated Parmesan cheese

2 tablespoons butter

Zucchini blossoms are a new addition to most American markets, but they've been used for centuries in Piemonte. With veal, sausage, parsley, and herbs, the dish is a great way to begin a meal.

This is one of the many dishes that Piedmontese cooks enhance with shaved truffles if they're available.

Gently wash the zucchini blossoms, pat dry, and set aside.

Soak the bread crumbs in the milk for 20 minutes and drain. Squeeze out the excess milk with your hands.

Combine the veal, sausage, salt, parsley, garlic, sage, and mint in a food processor, and pulse until mixed and finely chopped. Add the cheese, and soaked bread. Pulse the mixture a few more times to mix thoroughly.

Stuff the blossoms with the meat mixture. Melt the butter over medium-low heat, and sauté the blossoms, turning frequently. The dish is ready when the blossoms brown and the meat is thoroughly cooked.

Serve warm.

Zucchini in Carpione
Zucchini Marinated in Vinegar and Wine

4 SERVINGS

½ cup olive oil

1 pound zucchini, thinly sliced lengthwise

1 large white onion, thinly sliced

2 cloves garlic, thinly sliced

1 cup red wine vinegar

½ cup dry red wine

2 teaspoons whole black peppercorns

1 teaspoon whole allspice

4 bunches sage

3 bay leaves

In carpione means "in the mode of pickled carp." Today, carp is rarely pickled, but all kinds of items are prepared this way. They can be made in advance and served chilled. The zucchini recipe here is by far the most popular.

Heat the oil in a frying pan over medium heat. Brown the zucchini, drain, and blot the slices with paper towels. Sauté the onions in the same oil until translucent. Then add the vinegar, wine, and spices, and cook for 4 minutes on high heat.

Arrange the zucchini in a nonreactive baking dish large enough to hold the slices in a single, overlapping layer. Place the onions in an even layer on top of the zucchini. Pour in the vinegar mixture, and refrigerate for at least 5 to 6 hours.

Serve chilled or at room temperature.

Frittatine di erbe
Thin Herbed Omelets

These thin, herbed omelets are equivalent in size to silver dollar pancakes. Traditionally, they are made in the spring with wild greens like nettles, grape leaves, and poppy shoots, but we'll use herbs that are a bit easier to find.

4 SERVINGS

1 pound spinach, stemmed, cleaned, blanched, and chopped (about 1 cup)

30 mint leaves, chopped

3 fresh sage leaves, chopped

6 fresh basil leaves, chopped

1 tablespoon chopped fresh thyme

2 scallions, chopped

½ cup grated Parmesan or pecorino cheese

1 teaspoon salt

4 eggs, lightly beaten

Olive oil

Combine the spinach, mint, sage, basil, thyme, and scallions with the cheese and salt. Whisk the spinach mixture into the eggs.

Heat the olive oil in a nonstick frying pan over medium heat. Pour 1 tablespoon of the egg mixture into the pan and flip it when the edges begin to brown. The omelets are cooked when the egg has set. You can cook three or four omelets at a time, but be careful to leave space in between them so that they do not stick together. Add additional oil as needed.

Serve hot or cold.

Sformati
Vegetable Flans

The Piedmontese landscape is such a major producer of dairy and eggs that local cooks use them as the basis for many dishes. One creative way is in vegetable flans, savory vegetable custards, served as appetizers. The recipes offered here use common ingredients: bell peppers, spinach, and leeks. What happens to them after they're combined, however, is anything but common. They can all be served with Salsa Rossa Estiva (page 21) or Fonduta (page 24).

If you're starting to think that people drink heavy red wine with everything in Piemonte, flans are one exception; these dishes go perfectly with a Grignolino or Dolcetto—much lighter red wines that are just as much a part of Piemonte as Barolo and Barbera.

Sformato di Peperoni
Bell Pepper Flan

4 SERVINGS

3 yellow bell peppers, sliced

1 small onion, chopped (about 1/2 cup)

3 tablespoons butter

2 tablespoons all-purpose flour

2 cups milk

1/2 teaspoon grated fresh nutmeg

3 eggs, lightly beaten

1/3 cup grated Parmesan cheese

1 teaspoon salt

1/2 teaspoon freshly ground black pepper

Summer Red Sauce (recipe follows)

Preheat the oven to 350°F and grease a 9 x 5-inch loaf pan. Fill a larger pan with 2 inches of water for a bain-marie and set aside.

Spread the peppers and onion on a baking sheet and bake for about 30 minutes, or until the onion begins to brown at the edges. (If you're making Summer Red Sauce to go with this, roast the peppers for it at the same time.) Peel the peppers and cut the flesh into pieces. Puree the onions and peppers in a food mill or processor.

Make a besciamella (basic white sauce) by mixing the butter, flour, milk, and nutmeg as described in on page 107. Whisk in the pepper puree, eggs, cheese, salt, and pepper. Whisk constantly to make sure the eggs don't scramble. Pour the flan mixture into the prepared loaf pan and place it into the pan of water. Bake for 1 hour, until a toothpick stuck in the center comes out clean.

Remove from the oven and let cool. Run a knife around the edges of the flan and unmold it onto a plate.

Salsa Rossa Estiva
Summer Red Sauce

MAKES **2** CUPS

1 tablespoon olive oil

1 medium onion, chopped (½ cup)

2 cloves chopped garlic

1 sprig fresh rosemary

1 bay leaf

1 sprig fresh sage

6 leaves fresh basil

1 cup canned peeled,
crushed tomatoes

2 red bell peppers, roasted,
peeled, and seeded

Heat the olive oil over medium heat and sauté the onion and garlic. Tie the rosemary, bay leaf, sage, and basil together with string and add the bundle to the pan; cook, stirring, for 3 minutes more. Add the tomato and peppers, and cook for 20 minutes more.

Pass the mixture through a food mill or puree briefly in a food processor. Return the sauce to the pan, and cook over low heat for 10 minutes.

Serve warm.

a

Sformato di Porri
Leek Flan

4 SERVINGS

1 bunch leeks

1 tablespoon plus 1 ¼ teaspoons salt

3 eggs, separated

¼ cup grated Parmesan cheese

4 tablespoons butter

½ teaspoon freshly ground black pepper

Preheat the oven to 325°F. Grease a 9-inch square pan and fill a larger pan with 1 inch of water for a bain-marie.

Cut off the green part and root end of the leeks and discard. Halve the leeks lengthwise, and rinse them thoroughly to remove any sand. Bring a large pot of water to a boil with 1 tablespoon of the salt. Add the leeks and boil for 20 minutes. Drain and when cool enough to handle, squeeze any excess liquid from them. In a food processor, combine the leeks, egg yolks, cheese, butter, 1 teaspoon of the salt, and pepper, and puree. Remove from the processor, place in a large bowl, and set aside.

In a separate large bowl, beat the egg whites with the remaining ¼ teaspoon of salt until stiff peaks form. Carefully fold the egg whites into the leek mixture.

Pour the flan mixture into the prepared pan. Place it in the bain-marie. Bake for 40 minutes, or until a toothpick inserted in the center comes out dry.

Remove from the oven and let cool. Run a knife along the edge of the flan and unmold it onto a plate.

Serve warm with Salsa Rossa Estiva (page 21) or Fonduta (page 24).

Sformato di Spinaci
Spinach Flan

6 SERVINGS

2 pounds fresh spinach, or
1 (10-ounce) package frozen
chopped spinach, thawed

1 tablespoon plus 1 teaspoon salt

2 tablespoons butter

4 eggs, lightly beaten

1 cup whole milk

1 cup heavy cream

½ cup grated Parmesan cheese

½ teaspoon freshly ground
black pepper

½ teaspoon freshly ground nutmeg

Preheat the oven to 375°F. Grease six (4-ounce) ramekins and fill a pan large enough to hold all the ramekins with ¾ inch of water for a bain-marie.

Bring 4 quarts of water to a boil with 1 tablespoon of the salt. Boil the spinach for 1 minute, drain, and chop. Melt the butter over medium heat and sauté the spinach for 2 minutes.

Whisk together the eggs, milk, cream, cheese, remaining 1 teaspoon salt, pepper, and nutmeg. Stir in the cooked spinach.

Pour the mixture into the prepared ramekins. Because the flans will puff up in the oven, make sure the ramekins are only about three-quarters full. Place the filled ramekins in the bain-marie and place in the oven. Bake for about 40 minutes, or until a toothpick inserted in the center comes out clean.

Remove from the oven and let cool. Run a knife along the edges of the ramekins and unmold onto plates.

Serve warm with Salsa Rossa Estiva (page 21) or Fonduta (page 24).

Fonduta
Fondue

4 SERVINGS

1 pound fontal, fontina DOP, or a combination, cubed

2 cups whole milk

4 egg yolks, lightly beaten

ACCOMPANIMENTS:

Grissini

Bread cubes

Carrot sticks

Celery sticks

Truffle (optional)

Traditionally, **fonduta** is made with fontina D. O. P. from Valle d'Aosta (once a part of Piemonte and now an autonomous region), a pungent raw, cow's milk cheese from the high mountains. Another alternative is **fontal**, the same type of cheese, but made with pasteurized milk from outside Valle d'Aosta, which results in a milder flavor. Many people say that the best Fonduta is made with a combination of the two.

If you're not having a fondue party, consider using fonduta as a sauce over risotto, **sformati** (page 19), steamed asparagus, or other dishes.

Soak the cheese in the milk for 4 to 6 hours in the refrigerator.

Place the cheese mixture in the top part of a double-boiler over medium heat, and melt it slowly, stirring gently with a whisk. When the cheese is almost melted, gradually add the egg yolks, whisking continually to make sure they don't scramble. Keep stirring in the same direction until the fondue is no longer grainy or stringy and takes on a glossy finish.

To serve, immediately pour the finished fondue into a shallow bowl or fondue dish. Serve alongside plates of the grissini, bread cubes, carrots, and celery.

Shave truffles over the warm fondue for a luxurious enhancement.

Acciughe al Verde
Anchovies in Green Sauce

4 SERVINGS

1 cup fresh Italian parsley

3 cloves garlic

1 cup extra-virgin olive oil

2 hard-boiled egg yolks

2 tablespoons red wine vinegar

1/2 teaspoon crushed red pepper

1 teaspoon salt

12 salted anchovies,
rinsed and boned

This dish is a popular appetizer in country restaurants and is also commonly served for snacks, brunches, and even as a sandwich filling. It has traditionally played an important role in merende sinoire—informal summer afternoon meals taken by farmers during long harvest afternoons. It was always washed down with glasses of robust red wine—Barbera is what comes to mind here.

In a food processor finely chop the parsley and garlic. Add the oil, hard-boiled egg yolks, vinegar, red pepper, and salt, and pulse to mix. You should have a thick sauce, not a paste.

Arrange the anchovies flat on a platter and cover them with the sauce. Alternately, you can layer the fillets and sauce in a terrine—this occupies much less space on a crowded Piedmontese antipasto table.

Allow to rest for 6 to 8 hours in the refrigerator before serving, and serve at room temperature.

Bagna Cauda
Olive Oil and Anchovy Dip

4 SERVINGS

4 cups whole milk

4 heads garlic, separated
into cloves and peeled

3 ½ cups extra-virgin olive oil

12 salted anchovies, rinsed,
boned, and chopped

ACCOMPANIMENTS:

2 red or yellow bell peppers,
cut into strips

1 head cauliflower pieces, cut into
bite-size pieces and parboiled
(about 3 cups)

½ head Savoy cabbage, cut into strips
(about 3 cups)

3 Jerusalem artichokes,
peeled and cubed

2 beets, roasted, peeled and cubed

2 onions, baked and peeled

2 carrots, peeled, boiled, and sliced

3 potatoes, boiled and cubed

4 stalks cardoon, cut into 3"strips

1 loaf Italian-style crusty bread*

6 eggs

*Usually called a "Peasant loaf"
or a "Panella."*

When the Piedmontese think of their native cuisine, the first dish that comes to mind is Bagna Cauda. It has anchovies and garlic, the key peasant ingredients, and uses olive oil as the carrier of its flavor. On a cold winter's night, nothing is more satisfying than gathering around a warm pot of highly seasoned oil while watching the snow fall outside.

This is a strongly flavored dish for strong people. Whether you've just spent the day working in the fields or climbing in the Alps, this is a meal that will refresh your body and soul, and build friendships at the same time. Nineteenth-century cookbooks said that this dish should be accompanied by "rivers" of red wine. We list this dish as an appetizer but, for true fanatics, Bagna Cauda can be the centerpiece of a meal, too.

In a small pot, bring the milk to a boil. Lower the heat, add the garlic, and simmer for 1 hour. Remove the garlic from the milk and smash the cloves into a rough paste with a fork. Combine the garlic, oil, and anchovies in a saucepan over low heat and stir with a whisk until the anchovies dissolve and the liquid becomes almost creamlike.

Bagna Cauda is traditionally presented in a heatproof bowl, but a stainless steel or earthenware fondue pot makes an excellent presentation, too. Be aware that, if the heat gets too high, the garlic may burn.

Serve with a large platter of the vegetables and lots of bread. Diners can use pieces of bread to hold the vegetables and to mop up the dip.

At the end, when there's only a bit of sauce left, break the eggs into the dip and poach them over low heat. Many people say that bagna cauda with vegetables and eggs followed by fruit poached in wine (page 132) is a complete and classic meal.

Anchovies

In the Piedmontese kitchen, anchovies are a staple. They are strongly flavored and have good keeping qualities, two important attributes in the days before refrigeration.

Every cookbook, every class, and every expert in Italian cuisine we've ever talked to has stressed the importance of using whole salted anchovies, but testing recipes for this book, we made a discovery that borders on heretical: sometimes canned anchovy fillets taste better than salt-packed whole fish.

In our taste tests for these recipes, flat-packed anchovy fillets in olive oil gave results equal to salted whole fish. Our first choice is salted anchovies. These are traditional, and in most cases your best bet. But you can find good canned anchovies; they should be packed in olive oil, laid flat in the can, and should have a rich burgundy color. Choose the right anchovies and they will serve you well. Beware though: in our shopping, we noticed big differences in the way salted anchovies are stored. Look for ones that are dry and salt-coated rather than oozing liquid. If you use canned salted anchovies, drain them first. We don't recommend anything but the aforementioned two kinds. Anchovies packed in anything but olive oil, or rolled instead of flat, don't have as good flavor or consistency.

Insalata Russa
Potato and Tuna Salad

4 SERVINGS

1 tablespoon salt

4 large red-skinned potatoes

2 carrots, peeled

¹⁄₂ pound green beans, trimmed and cut into 1-inch pieces

1 cup fresh or frozen green peas, plus 3 tablespoons for garnish

³⁄₄ cup prepared marinated roasted red pepper strips, cut into 1-inch lengths

3 hard-boiled eggs, sliced

1 (6 ¹⁄₂-ounce) can tuna packed in olive oil, drained, and flaked

¹⁄₂ cup prepared marinated mushrooms, minced

1 cup Cipolline in Agro Dolce (see page 15), minced

2 ¹⁄₂ cups mayonnaise

*As the name suggests, **Insalata Russa** is not Piedmontese in origin. It came from nearby France where Russian aristocrats vacationed more than a hundred years ago. Ironically, in Russia, it's called "Italian Salad."*

*This is a potato salad, but not in the American sense; you won't see a scoop of **Insalata Russa** next to a sandwich but you might find a plastic container of it on a supermarket shelf. In restaurants, brightly decorated platters of **Insalata Russa** will be at the forefront of appetizer displays. Maria's mother always made it for guests or Sunday lunch. She took special pleasure in decorating it— there was invariably a "Wow!" when it was brought to the table.*

The version here uses marinated onions, mushrooms, and peppers—ingredients that are not universal, but favorites of Maria's family.

Bring 2 quarts of water to a boil with the salt, add the potatoes and carrots, reduce the heat to a simmer, and cook for 15 minutes. Add the green beans and simmer for 10 minutes more, until all the vegetables are fork tender. Drain the vegetables and peel the potatoes. In a separate small saucepan, simmer the peas in 2 cups of water until they, too, are fork tender (cook the peas separately so that they don't get crushed by the other items). When they are cool, cube the carrots and potatoes.

In a large bowl combine the vegetables, ¼ cup of the marinated peppers, 2 of the hard-boiled eggs, the tuna, marinated mushrooms, and cipollini with 1½ cups of mayonnaise, and mix gently so that the ingredients are all evenly coated yet remain solid. Transfer to a serving dish, spread the remaining mayonnaise over the salad, and decorate with the remaining peas, sliced egg, and marinated peppers. Refrigerate for at least 2 hours so that the flavors combine, and serve chilled.

Insalata di Trota
Trout Salad

4 SERVINGS

2 cups white wine

¼ cup plus 1 tablespoon white wine vinegar

1 onion, quartered

1 clove garlic

1 celery stalk, with leaves

1 bunch Italian parsley plus 2 tablespoons chopped

2 teaspoons salt

2 whole (1-pound) trout

1 cup plus 2 tablespoons extra-virgin olive oil

6 new potatoes, quartered

3 tablespoons capers, rinsed and drained

6 anchovy fillets

2 tablespoons chopped fresh parsley

4 raw artichoke hearts, thinly sliced*

2 cups mixed greens

1 cup cherry tomatoes

1 lemon, thinly sliced

Blanched asparagus tips can be substituted for artichokes in season.

This is a great hot-weather presentation for fresh trout.

To poach the trout: In a saucepan, bring 4 cups of water, ¼ cup of the vinegar, onion, garlic, celery, bunch of parsley, and 1 teaspoon of the salt to a boil for 1 minute, then reduce the heat to a simmer. Put the trout into the liquid and cook until barely done—no more than 10 or 12 minutes. Drain the trout, pat dry, and set aside to cool.

When the fish has cooled, carefully remove the head, tail, skin, and bones so that the fillets remain in at least 1-inch chunks. Drizzle 2 tablespoons of the remaining oil and 1 tablespoon of vinegar over the fish, and let it marinate in the refrigerator for at least 1 hour.

Bring 8 cups of water to a boil with the remaining 1 teaspoon of salt. Add the potatoes and cook until tender, then drain and cool.

For the dressing: Combine the remaining 1 cup of olive oil, the capers, anchovies, and remaining 2 tablespoons of parsley in a blender and puree until smooth.

To assemble the dish: Arrange the trout, potatoes, and artichokes in the center of a platter and pour a bit of the dressing over them. Surround them with the mixed greens and garnish with the cherry tomatoes and lemon slices.

Salame di Tonno
Tuna Salami

6 salted anchovies, rinsed and boned

2 (6 ½-ounce) cans tuna packed in olive oil, drained

½ cup chopped fresh Italian parsley

¼ cup dry bread crumbs

2 hard-boiled eggs

1 teaspoon salt

½ teaspoon freshly ground black pepper

1 tablespoon capers

1 tablespoon red wine vinegar

2 tablespoons olive oil

Cheesecloth

Kitchen twine

It's amazing how these same basic ingredients—canned tuna, anchovies, parsley, and capers—turn up in so many different forms. This is one of the most unusual—it isn't exactly salami in the technical sense, but it's shaped and sliced like one.

If you're serving another appetizer with a mayonnaise sauce, you can use that sauce instead of the one below.

Bring 6 quarts of water to a boil in a large saucepan. Combine 4 of the anchovies, the tuna, parsley, bread crumbs, eggs, salt, and pepper in a food processor, and pulse into a coarse paste. Put this mixture on a piece of cheesecloth and form into a 2-inch-thick salami. Roll the cloth tightly and tie the ends with kitchen twine. Place it in the boiling water, reduce the heat to a simmer, and cook, uncovered, for 20 minutes.

Prepare the sauce: Finely chop the remaining 2 anchovies and capers, and put them in a bowl. Add the vinegar and whisk in the oil, one drop at a time, until a paste forms.

Remove the salami from the pot and let it cool. Unwrap, slice, arrange on a serving dish, and drizzle with the sauce.

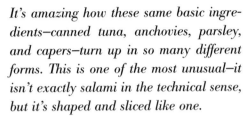

Insalata Capricciosa
Chicken and Ham Salad

4 SERVINGS

1 bulb fennel, trimmed

1 chicken breast (about 8 ounces)
boneless, skinless chicken breast,
poached

8 ounces cooked ham

4 ounces fontina cheese

1 small head radicchio
(about 4 ounces)

½ teaspoon salt

¼ teaspoon freshly ground
black pepper

¼ cup plus 2 tablespoons
mayonnaise

The crunchiness of fennel and radicchio in this salad will surprise those Americans like Brian, who complain endlessly that Piedmontese chefs overcook their vegetables.

Cut the fennel crosswise into ¼-inch strips. Cut the chicken, ham, cheese, and radicchio into strips of the same size. In a large bowl, toss all the chopped ingredients together with the salt and pepper. Mix in the mayonnaise and make sure all the ingredients are well coated. Serve cold.

Prosciutto in Gelatina
Ham Rolls in Aspic

6 SERVINGS

1 (6 ½-ounce) can tuna packed
in olive oil, drained

2 tablespoons capers,
rinsed and drained

2 hard-boiled eggs

½ cup mayonnaise

6 thin slices cooked ham
(prosciutto cotto)

4 cups chicken or beef broth*

4 tablespoons (4 envelopes)
unflavored gelatin

A favorite dish from Maria's childhood. This dish meant that guests were coming or a big holiday was about to be celebrated. Today, this dish is quite popular at **gastronomie**—*takeout shops that never fail to dazzle even the most jaded Italian shoppers.*

In a food processor, combine the tuna, capers, hard-boiled eggs, and mayonnaise, and process into a thick paste.

On a work surface, lay a slice of ham flat and put 2 tablespoons of the filling on one end. Roll up the ham around the filling, and set it in a nonreactive 13 x 9-inch dish.

Place the broth in a saucepan and sprinkle the gelatin over it. Let the mixture stand for 1 minute, until the gelatin softens. Stirring gently, warm the liquid over low heat until the gelatin is completely dissolved.

Pour the broth over the ham rolls and chill until the gelatin has set, about 2 to 3 hours.

Insalata di Carne Cruda
Raw Meat Salad

4 SERVINGS

1 pound boneless veal, trimmed of all fat and skin, minced

1 clove garlic, minced

2 tablespoons extra-virgin olive oil

½ teaspoon salt

¼ teaspoon freshly ground black pepper

1 ½ tablespoons lemon juice

When Brian sat down to his first meal in the Asselle household, to his surprise he saw a plate of raw veal. Traditionally, the meat in this salad was finely chopped, but when carpaccio became a popular dish, slices became more common.

Combine the meat, garlic, oil, salt, pepper, and lemon juice, and marinate for 15 to 20 minutes in the refrigerator. (If you are making this in advance, don't add the lemon juice until the very last minute, to make sure it doesn't cook the meat.) Serve chilled.

Brian Meets Raw Meat

When Brian first started visiting Piemonte in the mid 1980s, one of the culinary traditions that stood out most was the frequent consumption of raw meat. *Carne Cruda*—sliced or ground raw veal with olive oil, lemon, and raw garlic; and *salsiccia di Bra*—mildly seasoned tiny salami made from raw ground veal with added pork fat were both of note. They were served as antipasti in Maria's home at almost every meal. The raw veal was eaten as if it were cooked, except that it wasn't, and the little salami were broken open and spread like butter on bread.

Brian wanted the food that many Americans want at the start of a meal: salad. Now there is no shortage of good salad greens in Piemonte, but the Asselle family just wasn't into them. "Too hard to digest" was the explanation that was offered. At that time, Maria's father—who insisted that his stomach was too weak for all sorts of things, including most raw vegetables—ate raw meat with gusto. Indeed, to the Piedmontese, raw veal with extra pork fat added is considered an appropriate food for the frail and elderly.

It was obvious that Brian's perceptions of food needed some adjustment.

Vitello Tonnato
Veal with Tuna and Caper Sauce

This classic cold meat dish is great as an appetizer, for buffets, or as a main course on a hot day.

4 SERVINGS

1 tablespoon salt

1 carrot, peeled and roughly chopped

1 large onion, quartered

2 celery stalks, roughly chopped

2 bay leaves

1 (2-pound) boneless veal roast*

1 (6-ounce) can solid white tuna packed in olive oil

½ cup mayonnaise

1 cup extra-virgin olive oil

¼ cup lemon juice

2 tablespoons capers, rinsed and drained, plus extra for garnish

4 anchovy fillets, plus extra for garnish

¼ cup chopped fresh parsley

*You can use a pork loin roast instead if veal isn't available.

To prepare the veal: Bring 4 quarts of water to a boil with the salt. Add the carrot, onion, celery, and bay leaves, reduce the water to a simmer, and cook for 5 minutes covered. Add the veal and simmer, covered, for 1 hour. Turn the meat in the pot every 15 minutes or so to ensure that it cooks evenly. When it's done, remove it from the pot and let cool. Reserve the broth for a future use. It's great for soups and risotto.

For the tuna sauce: Combine the tuna, mayonnaise, olive oil, lemon juice, capers, and anchovies in a food processor, and blend to a smooth paste. Add the parsley and pulse several times.

To assemble the dish: Slice the meat thinly and fan out the slices on a platter. Evenly spread the sauce over the meat and garnish with additional capers and anchovies if you wish. Chill for at least 1 hour before serving, so the flavors can combine.

Lingua con Acciughe
Tongue with Anchovies

4 SERVINGS

2 celery stalks, roughly chopped

1 carrot, peeled and roughly chopped

3 cloves garlic

1 bunch parsley

2 tablespoons salt

1 (2-pound) veal tongue*

¼ cup wine vinegar

12 salted anchovies, rinsed and boned

1 cup olive oil

1 lemon, thinly sliced

1 cup prepared marinated mushrooms

Those who aren't tongue fans can substitute a veal roast.

This is another example of a cold sliced meat dish with an intense sauce. It's perfect as an appetizer or as an entree on a hot day.

To make the tongue: Put 4 quarts of water in a large pot with the celery, carrot, garlic, parsley, and salt, and bring to a simmer. Add the tongue, and cook for 1 hour. When the meat is fork tender, remove the tongue and immediately peel off the skin. (This will be easy now, but becomes difficult when the meat cools.) Sprinkle the tongue with the vinegar, let it cool, and slice it ¼ inch thick.

To make the sauce: Place the anchovies in a saucepan with the olive oil, and cook over a very low flame, stirring continuously. The anchovies will dissolve in the oil and form a sauce similar to Bagna Cauda (page 26).

Fan out the slices of tongue on a platter and cover the meat evenly with the sauce. Place a lemon slice over each slice of meat and garnish with the marinated mushrooms. Let the dish rest for at least 1 hour in the refrigerator before serving.

Primi Piatti

[PASTA, POLENTA, RICE, AND SOUP]

How often have you heard somebody say that "in Italy, every meal is a celebration?" With its fixed progression of courses and grand presentations, you can sense a feeling of festivity at almost any meal. Primi piatti signal the moment when the courses switch from small tidbits to full plates.

Basic ingredients like wheat and rice, when combined with a bit of water, broth, or egg, are converted to pasta and risotto dishes that are the backbone of the Italian diet. A portion of perfectly cooked Agnolotti (page 50), or a steaming mound of Risotto al Vino Rosso (page 65) tells us that this is the real thing, we really are eating in Italy, or at least among people who treat food with the same reverence as do Italians.

La Pasta

Basic Pasta Dough

Fresh pasta is a staple in Piemonte. Baked as lasagna, served with a wide range of sauces, or just a bit of butter and grated cheese, it shows up everywhere. Few households make fresh pasta often, but if you choose to, you'll turn an otherwise simple meal into a special occasion.

4 SERVINGS

1 cup all-purpose flour

2 eggs

3 tablespoons salt

With the flour, make a mound on a flat surface. Form a well in the top and break the eggs into it. Using a fork, immediately begin mixing them with small amounts of the flour. Soon the mixture will bind together enough to form a dough. Sprinkle a bit of flour on your work surface and knead the dough until it starts to become elastic, about 2 minutes Cut it into smaller pieces and use a rolling pin to flatten them into sheets.

This is the moment to bring out the pasta machine. Roll your sheets through each thickness several times changing to progressively thinner slots until you have the size you want. Then use the attachments to cut them into shapes. Sprinkle the finished pasta with a bit more flour and let it dry flat for an hour, or until it just begins to harden.

To prepare, bring 6 quarts of water to a boil with the salt and add the pasta. When the water returns to a boil, reduce the heat to a simmer and cook, stirring occasionally, for 3 to 4 minutes. The pasta is ready when the floury taste is cooked out but the texture is still al dente. Serve immediately.

Tajarin
Rich Egg Pasta

4 SERVINGS

2 cups all-purpose flour, plus additional for rolling and cutting

2 eggs

6 egg yolks

2 teaspoons olive oil

3 tablespoons salt

In Piemonte, eggs are used in astounding numbers. Legend has it that more than a dozen has been used in a single serving of pasta. In the name of healthy eating, we'll keep the number of egg yolks down, but not below what is common locally.

Traditionally, the dough is made using the well method: The flour is piled on a flat surface and a well or indentation is formed in the top. The eggs are put into the well and the flour is worked in with a fork. Today, it's far more common to do this in a mixer or food processor.

Put 1 cup of flour, the eggs and egg yolks in a mixer or food processor, and blend just to mix. As the dough starts to come together, add more of the flour and pulse a few more times. When all the flour is mixed in and the dough begins to form a ball, it is ready.

Remove the ball of dough from the bowl and knead it by hand on a well-floured surface until most of the moisture is absorbed and the dough is smooth.

Form into a flat sheet, and fold it over a couple of times so that it's narrow enough to fit into the pasta machine. Sprinkle it with more flour. Cover the pieces you aren't using with a damp towel so they don't dry out.

Flour the pasta machine's rollers, set it at the widest setting, and run the dough through it. Fold the dough over, back to its original thickness, and put it through the machine again. Repeat this process, making the settings thinner and thinner until your dough is as thin as possible. Lay the dough on a floured surface to rest for 10 or 15 minutes.

Set the pasta machine's cutter at medium width (the tagliatelle setting) and run the thin pasta sheets through. Be careful the strands don't stick together. Lay them on a floured surface in straight rows and let dry until they begin to harden, about 45 to 75 minutes.

To cook the pasta, bring 8 quarts of water to a boil with the salt. Add the pasta, stirring to make sure it doesn't stick or clump together. The pasta will be ready in 1 minute. Drain and serve immediately.

This fresh pasta is best served with simple sauces like Sugo Burro e Salvia (page 44), Sugo di Fegatini di Pollo (page 46), or Sugo di Carne (page 47).

Sugo Burro e Salvia
Butter and Sage Sauce

4 SERVINGS

¼ **cup butter**

2 sprigs fresh sage

This sauce is ideal for fresh pasta and very easy to make. Rosemary can be substituted for sage.

Melt the butter in a saucepan over medium-low heat until it begins to foam. Add the sage, stir a few times, and remove from the stove. Let rest for at least 10 minutes to infuse the butter with the herb. Remove the sage just before serving.

Serve over fresh pasta (page 40), with grated Parmesan cheese on the side.

L'Aja
Walnut Sauce

4 SERVINGS

½ cup cubed white bread, crusts removed

1 cup milk

4 ounces walnuts, chopped (about ½ cup)

4 cloves garlic

1 cup olive oil

1 teaspoon salt

½ teaspoon freshly ground black pepper

1 tablespoon butter

½ cup grated Grana Padano or Parmesan cheese

For most people in the United States, pasta sauce is red, except when it's green, but in Piemonte, it can be almost any color. L'aja is about as different from a red sauce as can be. While this is a perfect food processor or blender dish, it's also THE recipe to try if you have a mortar and pestle.

Soak the bread in the milk for at least 20 minutes. Make sure that none of the bread is dry and the milk is completely absorbed. Combine the soaked bread, walnuts, garlic, oil, salt, and pepper in a food processor and pulse until a puree forms.

To serve, pour the sauce on just-cooked pasta and toss with the butter and cheese.

Sugo di Fegatini di Pollo
Chicken Liver Sauce

The richness of chicken livers gives this sauce the substance to complement pasta and polenta.

6 SERVINGS

3 tablespoons butter

2 tablespoons olive oil

1 shallot, finely chopped

1 teaspoon finely chopped rosemary

8 ounces chicken livers, thinly sliced

¼ cup chicken broth

1 cup canned crushed tomatoes

¼ teaspoon freshly ground black pepper

½ teaspoon salt

Heat the butter and oil over medium heat and sauté the shallots and rosemary until the shallots are translucent. Mix in the chicken livers and cook, stirring, until the livers begin to turn golden. Add the broth and simmer, stirring occasionally, until the liquid has completely evaporated. Mix in the tomato, pepper, and salt, and continue cooking for about 15 minutes, or until the tomato has lost its raw flavor and the sauce has thickened.

Sugo di Carne
Meat Sauce

4 SERVINGS

¼ cup olive oil

1 medium onion, finely chopped (about 1 cup)

1 carrot, peeled and finely chopped (about ½ cup)

1 clove garlic, minced

1 sprig fresh rosemary

4 ounces ground veal

4 ounces ground pork

4 ounces canned crushed tomatoes

1 teaspoon salt

1/2 teaspoon freshly ground black pepper

If your idea of "meat sauce" is lots of toma-toes with a little meat, you're not thinking of the Piedmontese version. This sauce has tomato, but it's really about meat.

Heat the olive oil over medium heat and sauté the onion, carrot, garlic, and rose-mary, stirring. When the onion becomes translucent, add the veal and pork. Cook until the meat is well browned. Then add the tomatoes, salt, and pepper and reduce the heat to low. The sauce should barely simmer. Cook for at least 30 minutes, or until the raw taste is completely gone from the tomatoes and most of the liquid has evaporated.

Serve this sauce with Tajarin (page 42) or other pastas.

Tagliatelle Gialle e Verdi al Gorgonzola e Ricotta

Spinach and Egg Noodles with Gorgonzola and Ricotta

6 SERVINGS

¼ cup plus 3 tablespoons butter

4 ounces Gorgonzola cheese, crumbled

3 tablespoons heavy cream

1 cup fresh ricotta (about 5 ounces)

¼ teaspoon freshly ground black pepper

3 tablespoons salt

8 ounces dry egg tagliatelle

8 ounces dry spinach tagliatelle

2 tablespoons grated Parmesan cheese

Dry tagliatelle is easily available in most supermarkets, but this sauce is also great with fresh homemade pasta (page 40).

Melt 3 tablespoons of the butter in a saucepan over low heat until it begins to foam. Add the Gorgonzola cheese and heavy cream and cook, stirring, over low heat until the cheese is melted. Mix in the ricotta and pepper. Keep warm.

Bring 6 quarts of water to a boil in a large pot with the salt, and add the pasta. When the water returns to a boil, reduce the heat to a simmer and stir occasionally until the pasta is al dente.

Drain the pasta and combine it with the cheese sauce in a serving bowl. Toss with grated Parmesan cheese, and serve immediately.

Tagliatelle all'Uovo con Zucchini e Acciughe

Pasta with Zucchini and Anchovies

No vegetable is more of a special treat in Piemonte than zucchini with its blossoms. They are at their peak at about the same time as plum tomatoes. This combination makes a great sauce for fresh (page 42) or dried egg pasta.

4 SERVINGS

1 pound small zucchini with their blossoms

4 ripe plum tomatoes (about 6 ounces)

3 tablespoons olive oil

2 tablespoons butter

¼ cup fresh sage leaves

3 salted anchovies, rinsed and boned

3 tablespoons plus 1 teaspoon salt

¼ teaspoon freshly ground black pepper

1 pound egg tagliatelle

½ cup coarsely chopped fresh basil

3 tablespoons grated Parmesan cheese

Slice the zucchini about ⅛ inch thick. Set aside with their blossoms.

Bring 4 cups of water to a boil and immerse the tomatoes. They should stay in the boiling water no more than 30 seconds. As they cool, you should be able to peel them easily. When that's done, remove the seeds, squeeze out the liquid, and finely chop the remaining pulp.

Heat the olive oil and 1 tablespoon of the butter in a large skillet over moderate heat. Add the sage and anchovies, and cook, stirring, until the butter melts. Add the zucchini and blossoms; cook until the slices begin to brown at the edges. Stir in the tomatoes and add 1 teaspoon of the salt and the pepper. Remove half the vegetables and set aside.

Bring 6 quarts of water to a boil and add the remaining 3 tablespoons of salt. Put in the tagliatelle and reduce the heat to a simmer. Cook the pasta for 1 minute less than the length of time directed on the package, drain, and add to the vegetables in the skillet. Add the remaining tablespoon of butter and the basil. Place the tagliatelle in a serving bowl and pour the remaining vegetables on top. Serve with the grated Parmesan cheese.

Agnolotti
Piedmontese Ravioli

4 SERVINGS

Ravioli seems to have come to Piemonte from Liguria, where they were stuffed with greens, eggs, and cheese. As they moved north, however, leftover meat began to appear as a filling. In Langhe, these dishes are collectively known as **raviole**.

There are a number of legends about the origin of agnolotti. Some people argue that it derives from the ancient word for the tool—the **anolot**—*used to cut them into squares. Others say that they were once stuffed with* **agnello** *(lamb). And a different group maintains that the Marquis of Monferrato asked his chef to prepare a feast to celebrate the end of a long siege; since there was almost nothing left to eat, the chef combined the few remaining pieces of meat with some greens and stuffed these ingredients into pasta—and, of course, he made the dumplings as small as possible to be able to serve everybody. The chef was named Angeloto (Angelot, in Piedmontese dialect) so the dish became known as the* **piat d'Angelot**, *which later became* **agnolot**.

Regardless of the origin of their name, agnolotti are found all over Piemonte. In Torino and the richer plains, agnolotti are stuffed almost exclusively with meat. In Langhe, large quantities of greens, such as spinach, escarole, or cabbage, are added to the filling, and in some cases they are the main ingredient (see Agnolotti Verdi, page 52). In Langhe and Monferrato, you often find **agnolotti con il plin**, *small dumplings sealed by hand with a pinch (***plin*** in the Piedmontese dialect). They are small, irregular, and have a very thin skin, all characteristics that enhance the flavor of their filling. We recommend tasting them without sauce or with simple dressings, such as melted butter with sage or rosemary. A sauce made from the drippings of roasted meat is often used, too.*

FILLING:

1/4 cup butter

1/4 cup olive oil

1 clove garlic

1 sprig fresh rosemary

1 bay leaf

1/2 pound beef eye round

1/2 pound pork loin

1/2 teaspoon salt

1/4 cup beef broth

1 pound fresh spinach, stemmed and blanched

1/4 cup grated Parmesan cheese

2 eggs

1/4 teaspoon grated nutmeg

1/4 teaspoon freshly ground black pepper

DOUGH:

2 cups all-purpose flour

2 whole eggs

4 egg yolks

Melt 2 tablespoons of the butter with the oil, garlic, rosemary, and bay leaf in a pan over medium heat. Brown the beef and pork until as much of the surface as possible is golden. Season the meat with the salt, add 2 tablespoons of the broth, reduce the heat to low, and simmer, covered, for 1 hour and 15 minutes. Check the meat every few minutes and add a few table-spoons of broth if the pan becomes dry. When the meat is cooked through, remove it from the pot and let cool. Reserve the meat juices at the bottom of the pan; they make a great sauce.

In a food processor, blend the meat and spinach with the cheese, eggs, nutmeg, and pepper to a smooth paste. Set aside.

Prepare the pasta according to the instructions on page 40. Lay a sheet of pasta on a floured surface and place 1/2 teaspoon of filling about 1 inch from the edge. Continue by making rows of spoonfuls of filling, each about 2 inches apart. Cover the sheet of pasta dough with another and press the sheets together along the spaces between the filling bits. Cut out each agnolotto using a fluted pastry wheel. Make sure that the edges are well sealed. Put them on a floured surface and let dry in a cool place for a couple of hours.

To cook, bring a large pot of salted water to a boil. Add the pasta and cook for 3 to 4 min-utes. Remove them with a slotted spoon. (Don't use a colander—they may break.) Serve them dressed with Sugo Burro e Salvia (page 44), or with the strained juice of the roast and Parmesan cheese on the side.

p

Agnolotti Verdi con Ripieno di Verdure

Green Ravioli Stuffed with Vegetables

6 SERVINGS

FILLING:

2 potatoes

2 tablespoons butter

3 tablespoons grated Parmesan cheese

1 tablespoon plus ½ teaspoon salt

2 leeks, cleaned and chopped (1 cup)

1 cup chopped Savoy cabbage

1 bunch beet greens, stemmed (about 1 cup)

1 bunch escarole (about 2 cups)

At Maria's mother's family farm, in the hills near Dogliani in Langhe, these ravioli were occasionally served but her mother never dared make them in her own home. Her father, who came from Bra and grew up in Torino, considered these inferior to "real" agnolotti. For him agnolotti meant a meat, not a vegetable, potato, or rice filling. After years of hearing this, it was a pleasure to discover this lighter alternative to the richer meat-filled ones. Beet greens are used both to color the pasta and as a filling ingredient, but you can use spinach instead.

For the filling: Put the potatoes in a pot and cover them with cold water. Bring the water to a boil and cook until fork tender, about 20 minutes. Drain and peel while still warm and puree with a food mill or ricer. Mix the potatoes with the butter and cheese, and set aside.

Bring 8 cups of water to a boil and add the salt, leeks, cabbage, beet greens, and escarole. Cook for 3 minutes, or until the cabbage and leeks just begin to turn translucent. Drain well, let cool a bit, and finely chop. Combine the potatoes and chopped vegetables.

DOUGH:

1 pound spinach, stemmed and blanched (about 1 cup)

3 cups all-purpose flour

3 egg yolks

1 tablespoon olive oil

¼ teaspoon salt

SAUCE:

2 tablespoons butter

3 sage leaves

2 tablespoons grated Parmesan cheese

To make the dough: Combine the spinach, flour, eggs, oil, and salt using the Basic Pasta Recipe instructions on page 40.

Lay a thin sheet of pasta on a flat floured surface and place ½ teaspoon of filling about 1 inch from the edge. Continue by making rows of spoonfuls of filling, each about 2 inches apart. Cover the sheet of pasta dough with another and press the sheets together along the spaces between the filling bits. Cut out each ravioli using a fluted pastry wheel. Make sure that each edge is well sealed. Put them on a flat floured surface and let dry in a cool place for a couple of hours.

To cook, bring a large pot of salted water to a boil. Add the ravioli and cook for 3 to 4 minutes. Remove them with a slotted spoon. (Don't use a colander—they may break.) Serve them dressed with Sugo Burro e Salvia (page 44) and Parmesan cheese.

Gnocchi di Patate
Potato Gnocchi

4 SERVINGS

2 pounds Yukon Gold potatoes, scrubbed

2 tablespoons plus ½ teaspoon salt

1 tablespoon olive oil

2 egg yolks

1 ¼ cup all-purpose flour

This is the basic gnocchi recipe and the quality of the potatoes are key to its success. Maria's family has always found that the yellow ones from Entracque, the mountain village near Cuneo where they often vacationed, are the best. In our search for an American alternative, we have had goods results with Yukon golds.

Put the potatoes in a pot and cover them with cold water. Bring the water to a boil and cook the potatoes until fork tender, about 20 minutes. When they are cooked, drain and peel while they are still warm, then puree with a food mill. In a bowl, combine the potatoes, ½ teaspoon of the salt, the olive oil, and egg yolks. While stirring, add the flour 2 tablespoons at a time until the dough comes together. You will use about 1 cup of flour here. Turn the dough onto a floured surface and knead it until it starts to become elastic.

Flour both the work surface and your hands one more time, and divide the dough in half. Form the dough into ropes about ½ inch thick. Cut each rope into ¾-inch pieces. To give the gnocchi their characteristic ribbed shape, use your fingers to gently press them against the tines of a fork and then let them fall onto the work surface.

Bring 6 quarts of water to a boil with the remaining 2 tablespoons of salt. Add the gnocchi 10 or 12 at a time so the pot doesn't get crowded. As they rise to the surface, remove them with a slotted spoon and put them in a serving bowl. They are great with a fresh tomato-basil sauce, Fonduta (see page 24), or such cheeses as Gorgonzola and fontina.

Gnocchi della Val Varaita
Val Varaita-Style Gnocchi

4 SERVINGS

1 pound Yukon Gold potatoes (about 5 medium potatoes)

3 tablespoons salt

8 ounces fontina cheese, cut into very small cubes (about 2 cups)

1 cup all-purpose flour

3 tablespoons butter

¼ cup grated Parmesan cheese

*As far back as the tenth century and throughout the Middle Ages, Val Varaita was a place of refuge for people fighting the king of France and the Catholic Church. There, the Occitans—people who spoke the langue d' Oc dialect—made this dish and called it **ravioles**. In Italian they are called gnocchi from **gnocco** or "bump." This is another dish that began with a type of cheese found only in a small area—**Toumin del Mel**. Today, those who don't have access to that local cheese use fontina.*

Bring 4 quarts of water to a boil and add the potatoes and 1 tablespoon of the salt. Reduce the heat to a simmer and cook until the potatoes are fork tender. Drain and peel, then puree in a food mill or processor. Combine with the fontina cheese and flour and mix into a paste. Flour a flat surface and knead the dough for 5 minutes, or until it becomes elastic. Use your hands to roll the dough into long ropes about 1 inch in diameter. Cut the ropes into 1 ½ -inch pieces. Pinch the ends of each piece slightly so that they are shaped like small footballs.

Bring 6 quarts of water to a boil with the remaining 2 tablespoons of salt and add the gnocchi. Reduce the heat to a simmer and stir occasionally until the dumplings float to the surface. Put them in a serving dish and set aside; they can be kept warm in a 200°F oven, if need be.

Melt the butter in a small saucepan over low heat until it turns light brown. Pour over the gnocchi and sprinkle with the Parmesan. Serve immediately.

Calhette
Valdese-Style Gnocchi

4 SERVINGS

4 ounces pancetta, cubed

1 medium onion, finely chopped (about 1 cup)

2 cloves garlic, finely chopped

1 tablespoon olive oil

2 pounds Yukon Gold potatoes, peeled

¼ teaspoon freshly ground black pepper

½ teaspoon ground cinnamon

2 cups all-purpose flour

2 tablespoons butter

3 tablespoons grated Parmesan cheese

Calhette *comes from the western mountains: Val Chisone, Val Germanasca, and Val Pellice, where the Valdese—an Occitan Protestant religious minority—found refuge during the Middle Ages. That's why this dish is similar to the ravioles in Val Varaita (see page 66), another place they lived.*

Instead of cheese, onions and pancetta are mixed into the gnocchi dough. As always, ingredients for this dish vary from town to town. Sometimes versions use boiled potatoes, but the one we're offering here uses raw grated ones instead.

Heat a skillet over low heat, and place the pancetta, onion, and garlic in the skillet, cooking until the onion is translucent and the pancetta begins to brown. Set aside.

Grate the raw potatoes using the large holes of a box grater or a food processor with the grating attachment, drain them in a colander, then wrap them in a clean kitchen towel or cheesecloth and squeeze out as much liquid as possible.

Put the grated potatoes in a bowl and add the pancetta mixture, pepper, and cinnamon. Combine them and then add 1 ¼ cups of the flour. Knead the dough until it begins to become elastic. Using your hands, form egg-shaped balls and dredge them in the remaining ¼ cup of flour.

Bring 6 quarts of salted water to a boil in a large pot. Gently immerse the potato balls and lower the heat to medium or they may fall apart. Stir them gently and simmer, covered, for 30 minutes, or until they are firm all the way through and there's no raw potato taste.

A few minutes before the *calhette* are ready, melt the butter in a saucepan over low heat until it turns golden brown.

When the *calhette* are cooked, remove them with a slotted spoon and put them in a serving bowl. Dress them with the browned butter and the Parmesan cheese. Serve immediately with a young red wine, such as Grignolino or Dolcetto.

Gnocchetti di Ricotta con Funghi Trifolati

Ricotta Gnocchi with Mushrooms

4 SERVINGS

1 pound fresh ricotta cheese

4 ounces grated Parmesan cheese

2 eggs

2 egg yolks

1 cup all-purpose flour

¾ teaspoon freshly ground black pepper

1 tablespoon plus 1 teaspoon salt

1 tablespoon butter

3 tablespoons olive oil

2 cloves garlic, minced

8 ounces fresh porcini or shiitake mushrooms, thinly sliced

1 bunch parsley, minced (1 cup)

Unlike most gnocchi, these are not made with potatoes. Instead, the main ingredient is ricotta cheese, which reflects that milk has been both plentiful and important to Piedmontese cooks. Also worth noting is the use of porcini mushrooms, that grow in the wild in rural Piemonte. In the United States, we use fresh shiitake instead with great success.

Line a strainer with a piece of cheesecloth and drain the whey from the ricotta.

Combine the ricotta and Parmesan cheese, eggs, egg yolks, flour, ½ teaspoon of the pepper, and ½ teaspoon of the salt in a large mixing bowl, and stir until a dough forms. Turn the dough out onto a floured work surface and form into ropes ¼ inch thick. Cut the ropes into ½-inch pieces and roll them against the prongs of a fork as described on page 54. These will have the same shape but will be a bit smaller.

Melt the butter with 1 tablespoon of the olive oil over medium heat. Add the garlic, mushrooms, ½ teaspoon of the salt, and the remaining ¼ teaspoon of pepper and sauté for 5 minutes. Add the parsley and continue cooking until the garlic has started to turn translucent.

Bring 6 quarts of water to a boil in a large pot with the remaining 1 tablespoon of salt and 2 tablespoons of olive oil. Reduce the heat to medium and add the gnocchi. They will sink at first and will float to the surface when they're fully cooked. Remove them from the pot, drain, and combine with the mushroom sauce. Serve immediately.

p

Polenta
Polenta

4 SERVINGS

1 tablespoon salt

2 cups coarse-grained yellow cornmeal

p

Polenta is simply cooked cornmeal, once the staple diet of Piemonte's poor. Now it's served in Alpine resort towns, where large groups of friends and family gather to enjoy time together. Polenta requires a large group for another reason, too: you'll need help sharing the task of stirring.

In Piemonte, polenta is almost always made of coarsely ground yellow cornmeal. It's widely available in supermarkets here, usually located right by the flour and sugar, or with such cereals as oatmeal. We suggest you avoid both instant and roasted products. The instant never seems to develop a good flavor or texture, and roasted cornmeal has a taste that is completely different from the one we are looking for.

Traditionally, polenta was served right on a wooden table or board, and divided into portions with a cotton thread; but today, it's often served on plates. In either case, it is accompanied by cooked sausages, braised meats, or served with cheese and butter melted on top. We suggest serving it with Coniglio al Civet (page 85) or Merluzzo con Cipolle e Prezzemolo (page 78). Among the cheeses that suit polenta, are fontina and mild Gorgonzola.

While eating polenta is a feast, cleaning the pot can be a drag. However, if you fill it with cold water and let it soak overnight, the following morning the film attached to the pot will come off easily.

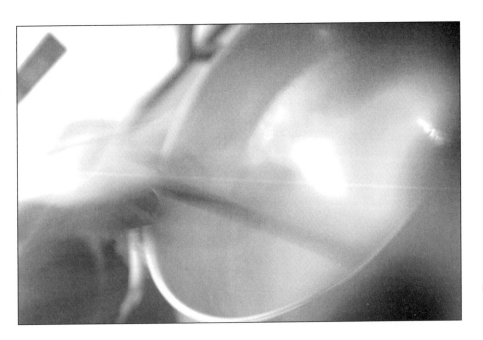

Bring 6 cups of water to a boil with the salt, in a heavy pot. Gradually whisk in the cornmeal, stirring constantly so lumps don't form. Reduce the heat to medium and switch to a wooden spoon for the stirring, which should remain continuous as the mixture thickens. (Be aware that if you stop, you'll have a solid mess.) The polenta is ready when it looks smooth and thick and comes away from the sides of the pan—about 40 minutes. Serve immediately.

Pasta al Forno
White Lasagna

6 SERVINGS

PASTA:

4 cups all-purpose flour

8 eggs

1 tablespoon salt

BÉCHAMEL SAUCE:

4 cups milk

1 tablespoon butter

¼ cup all-purpose flour

½ teaspoon salt

8 ounces Italian cooked ham, thinly sliced

8 ounces fontina cheese, thinly sliced

1 cup grated Parmesan cheese

½ teaspoon grated nutmeg

Piemonte is a land of dairy. In this rendition of lasagne, tomato sauce is replaced by a béchamel. While homemade pasta adds a nice touch to the dish, store-bought fresh pasta will be just fine.

Preheat the oven to 325°F. Grease a 9 x 13-inch baking pan with butter.

Prepare the pasta by incorporating the eggs with the flour as described in the basic pasta recipe on page 40. Use your pasta maker to roll it into thin sheets about 6 inches long.

Lay them on a flat, floured surface and let dry for about 30 minutes.

In the meantime, prepare the béchamel sauce according to the White Sauce instructions on page 107.

Bring 6 quarts of water to a boil with the salt. Add a few sheets of pasta at a time, cooking for 3 minutes. Drain, and line the bottom of the pan with a layer of pasta. Cover the first layer with ham, fontina cheese, and béchamel, and sprinkle with some of the Parmesan and the nutmeg. Repeat these layers until you have used up all the ingredients, finishing with the béchamel sauce and Parmesan cheese.

Bake for 45 minutes, or until the cheeses have completely melted and the top is golden brown. Serve hot.

Riso in Cagnon
Rice with Melted Cheese

4 SERVINGS

½ teaspoon salt

1 ½ cups arborio or Carnaroli rice

1 ½ tablespoons butter

3 sage leaves

½ pound Toma di Macagno or fontina, cubed

½ teaspoon freshly ground black pepper

3 tablespoons Parmesan cheese

*This is another dish from Biella, in the northeastern part of Piemonte. There the cheese used is **Toma di Macagno**, a local, aged raw-milk product. But fontina is a common substitute, even in Piemonte, and makes a delicious dish.*

Bring 4 cups of water to a boil with the salt. Add the rice, and lower the heat to a simmer. Cook for about 20 minutes, stirring occasionally, or until the rice is al dente. Drain.

Melt the butter with the sage in a small saucepan over low heat and cook, stirring, until the sage begins to wilt and the butter starts to brown.

Combine the hot rice, melted butter, and cheese in a serving dish and toss to combine and melt the cheese. Serve hot.

Note: Many people warm the serving dish before filling it with the rice to help melt the cheese. To do this, fill the dish with hot water, let stand for a few minutes, then pour out the water. Alternatively, put a bit of water in the dish and microwave it for a few minutes.

Paniscia

Rice with Salami and Beans

4 SERVINGS

1 cup dried borlotti or cranberry beans

2 tablespoons butter

¼ cup plus 3 tablespoons olive oil

1 stalk celery, diced (½ cup)

2 medium carrots, peeled and diced (about 1 cup)

1 cup shredded Savoy cabbage

1 teaspoon salt

½ frying chicken (about 1 ½ pounds)

1 pound beef shank

1 cotechino sausage

2 medium onions, thinly sliced

4 ounces soft, mild salami, such as cacciatorino, finely chopped

2 ½ cups arborio or Carnaroli rice

½ cup Barbera or other dry red wine

¼ teaspoon freshly ground black pepper

This is a famous dish from Biella and Novara in northeast Piemonte where **risaie** *(rice fields) fill the landscape. The name comes from* **panico** *(panic), a plant whose seeds were used originally to prepare it. Rice replaced panico, but the name remains. Traditionally, this recipe uses* **salam d'la duja**, *a soft pork salami (also known as* **cacciatorino**) *that is packed in fat in a terra-cotta container called a* **duja**. *This sausage can only be found locally but you can make this dish by using fresh high-quality* **cacciatorino** *salami. The other basic ingredient, borlotti beans, are an Italian variety that you can find in specialty stores. Otherwise, substitute cranberry beans.*

Like every recipe in Italy, this varies from area to area and family to family. Many use pork rind to cook the beans and broth. Marco Buzzio, originally from Biella and owner of the renowned Salumeria Biellese, the shop that makes sausages for the best restaurants in New York, suggested using **cotechino** *(see page 86), and substituting chicken and a beef shank for the pork rind.*

Put the dried beans in a bowl, cover with at least 3 inches of water, and let soak overnight. Rinse in cold water, drain, and set aside.

Melt 1 tablespoon of the butter with ¼ cup of the oil in a large pot over medium heat. Add the celery, carrots, cabbage, salt, and beans and cook, stirring, until the vegetables start to brown. Add the chicken and beef shank and cook until the chicken skin begins to brown. With a fork, prick the casing of the cotechino in few places and put it in the pot. Add 3 quarts of cold water, bring the stew to a simmer, and cook, covered, for about 1 hour. Remove the cotechino from the pot and continue cooking for 2 more hours. The meats should be thoroughly cooked and very tender. Remove from the broth and set aside. Reserve broth.

Place the remaining 2 tablespoons of oil, the salami, and onion in a large skillet over medium heat, and cook, stirring, until the onion is golden. Add the rice and stir with a wooden spoon until it's well coated with oil. Remove the skillet from the heat and pour in ¼ cup of the wine. Return the skillet to the heat and continue cooking it, stirring occasionally, adding more wine as necessary to keep the rice moist.

When all the wine has been absorbed, add ½ cup of the reserved broth. Cook, stirring, until the liquid is completely absorbed. Repeat this process until the rice is al dente. Remove the rice from the heat and stir in the remaining 1 tablespoon of butter. Set aside.

Meanwhile, warm up the cotechino by adding it back to the soup pot. When the rice is ready, remove the cotechino from the pot and cut it into ½-inch-thick slices.

To serve, put a mound of risotto on the plate, top with slices of cotechino, and sprinkle with freshly ground black pepper. Serve immediately.

Risotto alla Piemontese
White Risotto

As rice dishes spread across Piemonte, they incorporated local ingredients, but many share this method of incorporating liquid a bit at a time while stirring continuously. This dish can be enhanced with vegetables or mushrooms, and particularly complements Piemonte's local treasure, the truffle. This recipe can be the basis for any dish you can call your own.

4 SERVINGS

6 cups chicken broth

2 tablespoons butter

3 shallots, finely chopped

½ celery stalk, chopped (½ cup)

1 ½ cups arborio or Carnaroli rice

¼ cup dry white wine

¼ cup heavy cream

½ cup grated Parmesan cheese

½ teaspoon salt

¼ teaspoon freshly ground black pepper

Fresh white truffles if you can get them

Bring the broth to a simmer over medium heat in a saucepan. Melt the butter in a skillet over medium-low heat on the burner right next to the simmering broth. Add the shallots and celery and cook, stirring, until they begin to brown. Add the rice and stir until the grains are evenly coated with butter. Mix in the wine and cook, stirring, until it is completely incorporated. Add ½ cup of the broth and cook, stirring, until the rice absorbs it. When that happens, add another ½ cup of broth and cook, stirring, again until absorbed Repeat the process until all the broth is used up. By then, the rice should be cooked through and a creamy sauce will have formed. Taste a grain or two; the rice should be al dente, not crunchy or mushy. If it is crunchy, continue the cooking process with warm water. When it is al dente, stir in the cream, Parmesan cheese, salt, and pepper.

If you've managed to get a truffle, shave it over the risotto just before serving and don't be ashamed to make a bit of a show of the dish.

Risotto al Vino Rosso
Risotto with Red Wine

This dish combines red wine, one of Piemonte's best offerings, with risotto, one of its most basic cooking methods.

6 SERVINGS

6 cups beef broth

3 tablespoons butter

1 medium onion, chopped (about 1 cup)

1 tablespoon chopped fresh rosemary

2 cloves garlic, minced

4 ounces ground veal

2 cups dry red wine*

2 ½ cups arborio or Carnaroli rice

½ teaspoon grated nutmeg

¼ cup grated Parmesan cheese

*Barolo is the traditional choice— in fact, some cookbooks call this dish **Risotto al Barolo**—*but any robust red will do. Look for less expensive wines in the same family such as Barbera or Spanna, but any cabernet will do the job in a pinch.*

Bring the broth to a simmer in a large saucepan. Melt the butter in a large skillet over medium-low heat on the burner right next to the broth. Add the onion, rosemary, garlic, and veal, and cook, stirring, until the meat begins to brown. Add 1 cup of the wine and simmer until most of it has evaporated. Turn up the heat to medium-high and stir in the rice.

Add ½ cup of broth and stir continuously. As the liquid is absorbed, add another ½ cup of broth until a creamy sauce starts to form. Add the remaining wine and continue stirring while the rice is cooking. There should be no need to add any more broth, but if the rice is still crunchy, a bit more won't hurt. When the rice is fully cooked and a thick, creamy sauce has formed, add the nutmeg and cheese. Let it stand for a few moments to cool, and serve.

Risotto con Fonduta
Risotto with Cheese Sauce

Not only is cheese fondue a dish unto itself in Piemonte, it's also an important ingredient. Here, the combination of rich cheese and creamy risotto makes a substantial winter meal and a great foil for truffles.

4 SERVINGS

6 cups chicken broth

2 tablespoons olive oil

2 shallots, finely chopped

1 ½ cups arborio or Carnaroli rice

1 recipe Fonduta (page 24)

½ teaspoon salt

1 tablespoon butter

Shaved truffles (optional)

Bring the broth to a simmer over medium heat in a saucepan.

Heat the oil in a large skillet over medium heat on a burner right next to the broth and sauté the shallots in the olive oil until they just start to brown. Add the rice and stir until the grains are evenly coated with the oil. Add ½ cup of the broth and stir continuously until all the liquid is absorbed. Repeat the process until all the broth is used up. By then, the rice should be tender and a creamy sauce will have formed. Taste a grain or two, it should be al dente, not crunchy—continue the process with warm water if it isn't.

When the risotto is done, stir in half the Fonduta and the salt, and cook, stirring, for another 5 minutes. Remove it from the heat and mix in the butter.

To serve, place a mound of risotto in the center of the serving dish and make a well at the top of the mound. Fill it with some of the remaining Fonduta. Serve immediately and garnish with shaved truffles if you wish.

Risotto con Zucca
Risotto with Pumpkin

Pumpkin, the classic fall ingredient, adds wonderful flavor and deep color to risotto.

4 SERVINGS

2 large onions, 1 quartered and 1 chopped

1 large carrot, peeled and roughly chopped

1 red or yellow bell pepper, seeded and cut into strips

1 teaspoon salt

½ teaspoon freshly ground black pepper

3 cups cooked butternut squash or pumpkin

4 cups chicken broth

1 tablespoon butter

1 tablespoon chopped fresh rosemary

½ teaspoon freshly grated nutmeg

2 cups arborio or Carnaroli rice

¼ cup grated Parmesan cheese

Preheat the oven to 325°F and grease a baking sheet with olive oil. Spread the quartered onion, carrot, and bell pepper on the greased baking sheet. Sprinkle with the salt and pepper. (If your pumpkin isn't already cooked, include that, too.) Bake for 40 minutes, or until all the vegetables are fork tender and have begun to brown. Let cool. Combine the pumpkin, onion, carrot, and bell pepper with the cooked squash in a food processor, puree, and set aside.

Bring the broth to a simmer in a saucepan. Melt the butter in a heavy frying pan over medium-low heat and add the chopped onion, rosemary, and nutmeg. Cook, stirring, until the onion becomes translucent. Turn the heat up to medium, and stir in the rice. Add ½ cup of the broth and cook, stirring, until the rice absorbs it. When that happens, add another ½ cup of broth and cook, stirring, again until it's absorbed. After half the broth is used up, add the puree to the remaining warm liquid and stir to combine. Continue the risotto cooking process with this mixture. By the time the liquid is used up, the rice should be cooked through and a creamy sauce will have formed. If the rice isn't yet fully cooked—taste a grain or two, it should be al dente, not crunchy—continue the process with warm water. Otherwise, remove it from the heat, mix in the grated cheese, and serve immediately.

Torta di Riso
Rice and Vegetable Cake

This savory cake of rice and vegetables makes a perfect side dish or snack. When you make the risotto with vegetable broth, it's completely vegetarian, too.

8 SERVINGS

6 tablespoons butter

8 cups meat or vegetable broth

1 medium onion, finely chopped (about 1 cup)

3 cups arborio or Carnaroli rice

1 ½ cups blanched chopped spinach, or 1 (10-ounce) package frozen chopped spinach

3 eggs, lightly beaten

1 ½ cups grated Parmesan cheese

1 teaspoon salt

½ teaspoon freshly ground black pepper

Preheat the oven to 325°F. Grease a 2-quart baking dish with 2 tablespoons of the butter.

Bring the broth to a simmer. Melt 1 tablespoon of the butter over medium heat in a frying pan next to the pot of simmering broth. Add the onion and cook, stirring, until it becomes translucent. Stir in the rice until every grain is coated with butter. Add ½ cup of broth to the rice. It should be quickly absorbed. As this happens, add the broth by ¼ cupfuls until a creamy sauce starts to form.

In a separate pan, melt 2 tablespoons of the butter over medium-low heat and sauté the spinach until it begins to brown at the edges.

Combine the cooked rice, spinach, eggs, cheese, salt, and pepper in a large bowl. Work quickly to keep the eggs from scrambling.

Pour the rice mixture to the prepared dish. Cover with the remaining cheese and dot with the remaining tablespoon of butter, and bake for 1 hour, or until a toothpick inserted in the center comes out dry and the top begins to brown. Serve warm.

Zuppa Valdese
Breadstick Soup

4 SERVINGS

4 cups beef or veal broth

1/3 head Savoy Cabbage, cut in strips (about 2 cups)

1 tablespoon butter

4 Grissini (page 12), each broken into 4 pieces

1/4 cup grated Parmesan cheese

1/2 teaspoon grated nutmeg

The Valdese are one of the minorities that sought refuge in the mountains of Piemonte during the Middle Ages. Persecuted both for their minority status and religious beliefs, they established themselves mostly in the western valleys of Val Chisone, Val Germanasca, and Val Pellice. Valdese cooking is based on simple ingredients: potatoes, polenta, bread, milk, cheese, eggs.

Once upon a time this soup was prepared for special holidays and occasions. Its local name, **barbetta,** *derives from the name used for Valdese preachers who were called barbet for their characteristic beard* **(barba).**

Bring the broth to a simmer over medium heat and add the cabbage; cook for 20 minutes, stirring occasionally, or until tender. Spread the butter on the grissini. Divide the grissini between four bowls. Sprinkle a tablespoon of cheese in each bowl. To serve, place a bowl at each table setting and ladle 1 cup of the warm broth and cabbage into each bowl.

Zuppa di Pane, Patate, e Rape
Bread, Potato, and Turnip Soup

Turnips aren't common in Italian cooking, but they thrive in the cool mountain air of Piemonte.

6 SERVINGS

1 large turnip, peeled and sliced

3 Yukon Gold potatoes, peeled and sliced

2 teaspoons salt

2 cups cubed stale bread

2 tablespoons butter

4 cups beef broth

2 tablespoons grated Parmesan cheese

Bring 8 cups of water to a boil and add the turnip, potato, and salt. Reduce the heat to a simmer and cook for 20 minutes, or until the vegetables are fork tender. Drain and set aside.

Toast the bread cubes until golden brown. You can do this in either a toaster oven or a regular oven at 350°F for about 15 minutes. Divide the bread cubes between six soup bowls.

Melt the butter in a frying pan over medium-low heat and sauté the vegetables until golden brown. Add them to the bowls with the bread.

Heat the broth in a saucepan or microwave, and pour it over the bread and vegetables just before serving. Finish by sprinkling each portion with grated cheese.

La Cisrà

Chickpea Soup

8 SERVINGS

2 tablespoons olive oil

4 ounces pork fatback,
cut into small cubes

1 medium onion, chopped
(about 1 cup)

1 leek, chopped (about 1 cup)

5 cloves garlic, chopped

1 large celery stalk, chopped
(about ½ cup)

3 medium Yukon Gold potatoes,
peeled and cubed (about 2 cups)

1 large carrot, peeled and sliced
(about 1 cup)

½ large turnip, peeled and sliced
(about 1 cup)

8 ounces fresh mushrooms, chopped
(about 2 cups)*

1 cup chopped savoy cabbage

2 (15 ½-ounce cans) chickpeas,
rinsed and drained

1 sprig fresh rosemary

4 or 5 leaves fresh sage

3 bay leaves

2 teaspoons salt

1 teaspoon freshly ground
black pepper

Piedmontese cooks love big pots on the stove; stews, roasts, and soups, too. On cold, foggy winter days, nothing is more satisfying. This one, from Asti, is a classic of the genre.

Heat the oil in a large soup pot over medium heat, and brown the fatback. When the edges of the pork are golden, add the onions, leeks, garlic, celery, potatoes, carrot, and turnip. Cook, stirring, until the onions are translucent. Mix in the mushrooms and cabbage, and cook until the potatoes begin to brown at the edges. Add 6 cups of water, turn the heat to high, and bring to a boil. Put in the chickpeas, rosemary, sage, bay leaves, salt, and pepper and reduce the heat to medium. Simmer, covered, for 1 hour, stirring occasionally. Remove the rosemary, sage, and bay leaves before serving.

Serve hot with breadsticks (page 12).

*Try to find porcini, but shiitake or even portobello will work, too.

Cumaut
Cream of Pumpkin Soup

6 SERVINGS

2 tablespoons salt plus
1 teaspoon salt

2 pounds pumpkin, cut into chunks

2 medium Yukon Gold potatoes

1 whole onion, peeled

1 whole carrot, peeled

1 cup milk

½ teaspoon freshly ground
black pepper

2 tablespoons butter

1 teaspoon dried sage

Imagine a cold winter's dinner in the Alps. There might not be much available, but you'd have some pumpkin, potatoes and onions. Of course there'd be milk and butter—this is Piemonte! And a few dried herbs, too.

Bring 6 quarts of water to a boil and add the salt, pumpkin, potatoes, onion, and carrot. Reduce the heat to medium-low and simmer, covered, until the pumpkin and carrot are fork tender, about 30 minutes. Remove from the pot. Peel the pumpkin and potatoes. Puree the vegetables with a food mill or processor, and stir in the milk, salt, and pepper.

Melt the butter in a large saucepan over low heat, add the sage, and cook, stirring, until the butter has become infused with the sage, 2 to 3 minutes. Add the pureed vegetables and simmer, stirring occasionally, until the soup is warm and the flavors are combined.

Serve immediately.

Carne e Pesce

[MEAT & FISH]

In a land-locked region defined by its fertile soil, the Piedmontese have always been dependent on their livestock for sustenance. Meat and dairy are the mainstays of their diet, and wool has been an important rural industry for many centuries. Combine this with the cold mountain climate and you have the perfect backdrop for great meat dishes. Those barnyard staples, rabbit and chicken, play an important role, too. Without a coast, however, Piemonte has little tradition of seafood cookery, but three fish—salt cod, anchovies, and fresh trout—have made their way into local kitchens.

Long, slow cooking is the method of choice and one rarely finds a Piedmontese stir-fry. However, the cooking times shouldn't deter you—once the dish is on the stove or in the oven, it needs scant attention. For the effort of an occasional stir, you'll be rewarded with the fragrance of a great meal on the way.

Merluzzo in Salsa Verde
Salt Cod in Green Sauce

4 SERVINGS

1 ½ pounds boneless salt cod

1 cup all-purpose flour

½ teaspoon ground white pepper

2 cups plus 2 tablespoons olive oil

1 bunch fresh Italian parsley, chopped (about 1 cup)

3 cups chopped fresh spinach leaves, or 1 (10-ounce) package frozen chopped spinach

½ cup chicken broth

Salt cod (baccalà) is a magical food; it's strange looking with an even stranger smell, yet somehow it becomes an elegant meal with just a bit of help from the cook.

Rinse the salt off the surface of the fish and then, soak the salt cod in a nonreactive dish for 3 days, changing the water every 12 hours or so. This lengthy soaking makes a big difference in the tenderness of the fish.

Combine the flour and pepper. Cut the fish into 1-inch strips, pat them dry and dredge them with the flour mixture. Heat 2 cups of the oil in a skillet over high heat. It should be about ½ inch deep. Fry the cod in the oil until golden and drain on paper towels.

Heat the remaining 2 tablespoons of oil in a skillet over medium heat. Add the parsley and cook for about 5 minutes, then add the spinach. When the spinach wilts, pour in the broth and cook, stirring, until the liquid has evaporated.

Gently toss the cod and spinach together, and serve with boiled or mashed potatoes, or Polenta (page 58).

Buying Salt Cod

Salt cod isn't something that's native to Piemonte, or even Italy. It's historically a trade item with origins in the north Atlantic, but before the days of refrigeration and trucking, this was the only fish that most people away from the ocean could find in the markets.

If you spend time in many ethnic grocery shops, you're sure to spot the silver and white crumbly item that Italians call baccalà. People who are curious about foods are always lured to them but, all too often, their dishes wind up failures. Why? The quality of what they buy.

We are always tempted by the pieces that look the most like whole fish, but they turn out to be bony and leathery. Instead, look for thick filets that resemble white blocks. We urge you to buy some whenever you see quality fish offered. Salt cod lasts for months and, when the right piece is properly prepared, its flavor beats that trucked-in "fresh" stuff by a long mile.

Merluzzo con Cipolle e Prezzemolo

Salt Cod with Onions and Parsley

This is similar to Merluzzo in Salsa Verde (page 76), but with a richer tomato-based sauce that makes it a perfect fish accompaniment for Polenta (page 58).

4 SERVINGS

1 ½ pounds boneless salt cod

2 tablespoons all-purpose flour

¾ cup olive oil

3 scallions, chopped (about ½ cup)

2 cloves garlic, minced

1 medium onion, thinly sliced

1 large leek, sliced (about 1 cup)

1 bunch fresh Italian parsley, chopped (about 1 cup)

3 tablespoons capers, rinsed and drained

4 fresh sage leaves

¼ cup tomato paste

1 ½ cups milk

Rinse and soak the cod according to the instructions on page 76. Dry the cod with paper towels and dust with the flour.

Heat ½ cup of the oil in a heavy skillet and fry the cod until golden brown. Drain and set aside.

Heat the remaining ¼ cup of olive oil in a large skillet over medium heat and add the scallions, garlic, onions, and leeks, cooking until the edges of the onions begin to brown. Mix in the parsley, capers, and sage, and cook, stirring, until the parsley wilts. Add the tomato paste and milk, and stir until well combined.

Add the salt cod and simmer over low heat for 5 more minutes, or until the sauce is warmed through. Serve immediately.

Merluzzo con Patate
Salt Cod with Potatoes

This simple dish incorporates salt cod (baccalà), potatoes, and white wine.

2 SERVINGS

Rinse and soak the cod according to the instructions on page 76.

1 pound boneless salt cod

2 cups white wine

1 bay leaf

1 tablespoon whole black peppercorns

1 pound red new potatoes, quartered

Melted butter or olive oil

Combine the white wine, bay leaf and peppercorns with 2 cups of water, and bring to a boil in a large pot. Add the fish and potatoes, and reduce the heat to a simmer. Cook for 45 minutes, or until the potatoes are fork tender. Drain.

While they're still warm, quarter the potatoes and arrange them on a plate. Cover with the cod pieces. Serve with melted butter or olive oil drizzled on top.

c

Trota al Burro

Sautéed Trout

4 SERVINGS

4 (8-ounce) whole trout, cleaned
(fillets are fine too)

¼ cup all-purpose flour

2 tablespoons butter

3 fresh sage leaves

1 teaspoon salt

Piemonte's mountain streams are rich with trout. Butter is the chosen cooking medium and is responsible for the golden brown crispiness of its skin.

Wash the trout well both inside and out, and pat dry with a paper towel. Dredge the fish with the flour and shake off any excess.

Melt the butter in a skillet over medium-low heat and add the sage. When the leaves are coated with melted butter add the trout. Cook the fish on one side until the edges are golden brown—about 5 minutes. Turn with a spatula, season the browned side of the trout with the salt, cover the pan, and cook for about 5 more minutes, or until the flesh is cooked through. Serve warm.

Bocconcini di Pollo alle Erbe e Limone

Braised Chicken with Herbs and Lemon

4 SERVINGS

4 (4-ounce) boneless chicken breasts, cut into thirds

½ cup plus 1 tablespoon all-purpose flour

3 tablespoons olive oil

¼ cup chopped fresh Italian parsley

1 tablespoon finely chopped shallot

1 large stalk celery, chopped (about ½ cup)

1 tablespoon chopped fresh sage

1 clove garlic, chopped

1 teaspoon grated lemon peel

1 teaspoon fresh thyme

1 teaspoon fresh marjoram

2 cups dry white wine

1 tablespoon lemon juice

3 tablespoons capers, rinsed and drained

Made with boneless breasts, this is a more refined dish than the other chicken dishes included here. It also works well with pork or veal cutlets.

Pound the chicken breasts into thin cutlets. Dredge the cutlets in ½ cup of the flour. In a skillet, heat the oil over high heat and fry the chicken until barely golden. Set them aside. In the same pan, sauté the parsley, shallot, celery, sage, garlic, lemon peel, thyme, and marjoram, over moderate heat for 2 minutes. Pour in the white wine and bring to a simmer, stirring and scraping the brown bits from the pan. Sprinkle the remaining tablespoon of flour over the liquid, whisking to make a thick sauce. Return the chicken to the pan and let it warm through. Stir in the lemon juice and capers. Serve immediately.

If you reheat this dish, add a bit of extra wine and lemon to the sauce for moisture.

Pollo con Peperoni
Chicken with Peppers

4 SERVINGS

¼ cup olive oil

1 large onion, chopped (about 1 cup)

2 carrots, chopped (about 1 cup)

2 stalks celery, chopped (about 2 cups)

2 sprigs fresh rosemary

2 cloves garlic, chopped

2 ounces pancetta or Italian salami, chopped

1 (2- to 2 ½-pound) chicken, cut into pieces, skin removed

1 cup all-purpose flour

4 whole cloves

1 cinnamon stick

1 teaspoon salt

½ teaspoon freshly ground black pepper

4 large red or yellow bell peppers, seeded and coarsely chopped (about 3 cups)

1 cup canned crushed tomatoes

2 cups dry white wine

2 tablespoons wine vinegar

¼ teaspoon ground nutmeg

Piedmontese gardens produce wonderful bell peppers. They can be cooked by themselves (page 106) or with meat. This recipe pairs them with chicken.

Heat the oil in a large skillet over medium heat. Sauté the onion, carrot, celery, rosemary, garlic, and pancetta until the onion is translucent. Dredge the chicken in the flour and add it to the vegetables in the pan. Then add the cloves and cinnamon stick, and sprinkle with salt and pepper. When the chicken is golden brown, add the peppers, tomato, and 1 cup of the wine. Cook over medium heat for about 30 minutes, covered. Stir occasionally, adding ½ cup of white wine each time, making sure the dish isn't either too dry or too soupy. About 5 minutes before the dish is ready, add the vinegar and nutmeg. Simmer until the peppers are fork tender, and the sauce is thick.

Serve immediately.

Pollo alla Cacciatora
Hunter's-Style Chicken

4 SERVINGS

1 cup olive oil

1 medium onion, coarsely chopped (about 1 cup)

1 (3-pound) roasting chicken, cut into pieces

½ cup all-purpose flour

1 cup dry white wine

1 teaspoon salt

1 (28-ounce) can peeled, crushed tomatoes

2 tablespoons fresh rosemary

1 tablespoon chopped fresh basil

2 bay leaves

4 cloves garlic, minced

½ teaspoon freshly ground black pepper

*This is the Piedmontese version of the classic Italian dish, **Pollo alla Cacciatora** ("chicken in the style of the hunter's wife"). The method here is a bit different than most American recipes and makes a surprisingly mild dish.*

In a pan large enough to hold all the ingredients, heat ½ cup of the oil and sauté the onions until they begin to brown, about 15 minutes. Remove the onions and set aside.

Heat the remaining oil over medium heat. Dredge the chicken pieces in the flour and sauté them until the skin is golden brown. Add the white wine and salt, and simmer for 15 minutes, scraping any brown bits at the bottom of the pan and making sure they're all dissolved. Add the tomato, rosemary, basil, bay leaves, garlic, pepper, and the reserved onions. Cook for 15 minutes more at a high simmer. Serve hot.

C

Fagiano in Salsa di Fegatini
Pheasant in Liver Sauce

This is a traditional method for preparing a classic game bird, which often uses the liver. This may be a bit of work, but it's worth the effort. Pheasant liver is difficult to find, but chicken liver substitutes nicely.

3 TO 4 SERVINGS

2 tablespoons butter

3 tablespoons olive oil

2 tablespoons minced sage

1 clove garlic, finely chopped

2 ounces pancetta, coarsely chopped

2 teaspoons salt

1 (2- to 3-pound) pheasant, cut into serving pieces

²⁄₃ cup plus 2 tablespoons dry white wine

2 chicken livers, chopped

1 tablespoon lemon juice

½ teaspoon red pepper flakes

Melt the butter with the oil in a large pan over medium heat. Add the sage, garlic, pancetta, and salt and sauté until the edges of the pancetta begin to brown. Add the pheasant, turning frequently to brown evenly. Reduce the heat to low, add ²⁄₃ cup of the wine, and simmer, covered, for 1 hour. Remove the bird from the pot. Stir in the chicken liver, remaining 2 tablespoons of wine, lemon juice, and red pepper flakes. Return the pheasant to the pot, and simmer, covered, for 30 minutes.

Antipasti, clockwise from top left: Ham in Aspic (*Prosciutto in Gelatina*), Anchovies in Green Sauce (*Acciughe al Verde*), and Sweet-and Sour Onions (*Cippoline in Agro Dolce*).

Piedmontese bread and Breadsticks (*Grissini*).
Opposite page: Anchovies in oil, top; and in salt, bottom.

Pureeing potatoes for gnocchi using a foodmill.

Rolling out pasta dough, top, and cutting it into *Tajarin*, bottom.

Pasta with Meat Sauce (*Tajarin con Sugo di Carne*).

Gnocchi with Butter and Sage Sauce (*Gnocchi con Sugo Burro e Salvia*).

Classic Piedmontese vegetable dishes: Fried Carrots (*Carote Fritte*), left; and Sautéed Spinach (*Spinaci al Burro*), right.

Coniglio al Civet
Civet of Rabbit

This "Civet," a strongly seasoned game stew (boar and hare can also find their way into the pot), is a classic example.

4 SERVINGS

1 (2-pound), rabbit, cut into pieces

1 (750-milileter) bottle dry red wine

1 carrot, roughly chopped (about 1 cup)

1 celery stalk, roughly chopped (about 1 cup)

1 medium onion, roughly chopped (about 1 cup)

1 sprig fresh rosemary

1 bay leaf

2 whole cloves

¼ cup olive oil

½ teaspoon salt

¼ teaspoon freshly ground black pepper

Combine the rabbit, wine, carrot, celery, onion, rosemary, bay leaf, and cloves in a nonreactive container. Mix well to make sure all the meat is coated, and let marinate, covered, in the refrigerator for 24 hours.

Drain the meat and vegetables, and separate them, reserving the marinade. Finely chop the vegetables (a food processor is useful here). Heat the oil in a large pan over medium heat and brown the chopped vegetables. Raise the heat to high and add the rabbit, stirring frequently, for about 5 minutes until browned. Season with the salt and pepper. Add the marinade to the pan and lower the heat to a simmer. Cook uncovered for 1 hour. Remove the rabbit and set aside.

Continue cooking the liquid until it reduces to a thick sauce. Remove from the heat, and pass it through a food mill or puree in a food processor.

Arrange the rabbit on a platter and pour the sauce over it to serve.

Cotechino
Boiled Pork Sausage

4 SERVINGS

1 (1 ½-pound) cotechino sausage

1 (750-milileter) bottle dry white wine

2 bay leaves

1 tablespoon whole black peppercorns

Cotechino isn't the easiest sausage to find in the U.S., but it's often available in Italian specialty stores, and from suppliers on the Internet. In Italy, it's served in restaurants as a hot appetizer and at home with mashed potatoes as a main course during the winter.

Pierce the cotechino with a fork and marinade it in the white wine for 6 hours. The wine should completely cover the meat. Remove from the wine and put into a pot with 2 quarts of cold water. Bring to a boil over high heat and cook for 10 minutes. Remove from the heat and discard the water. Add 8 cups of fresh water, the bay leaves, and the peppercorns, and bring to a low simmer. Cover and cook for 2 hours.

Slice the cotechino and serve warm over mashed potatoes.

Lombo di Maiale alle Nocciole

Pork Loin with Hazelnut Sauce

Hazelnuts aren't just for sweets. Here they form a sauce for roast pork.

Preheat the oven to 350°F.

6 SERVINGS

2 tablespoons butter

3 tablespoons olive oil

1 (3-pound) pork loin roast

3 cloves garlic, chopped

1 sprig fresh rosemary

2 bay leaves

1 cup heavy cream

1 cup beef broth

1 teaspoon salt

½ teaspoon freshly ground black pepper

3 cups hazelnuts, toasted and finely chopped (4 ounces)

Truffle shavings (optional)

In a roasting pan over medium-low heat, melt the butter and heat the oil. Brown the pork with the garlic, rosemary, and bay leaves. Turn the roast frequently to make sure it browns as evenly as possible. Add the cream, broth, salt, and pepper.

Put into the oven and cook until a meat thermometer reads 155°F (this means it's ALMOST done). Remove from the oven, set the pork aside, and discard the rosemary and bay leaves. Add the hazelnuts to the remaining liquid. Slice the roast ¼ inch thick, return the slices to the pan, and cover with the sauce. Return to the oven for 5 minutes to heat the whole dish completely.

Garnish with the shaved truffle and serve immediately.

Maiale al Latte

Pork Roast Braised in Milk

Cooking pork in milk changes the texture of the meat in remarkable ways. During a long, gentle braising, the milk imparts a unique tenderness.

Combine the pork roast, milk, garlic, rosemary, salt, and pepper in a heavy pot or Dutch oven. Place in a cold oven. Turn the oven to 225°F and bake for 4 hours, starting your timing after the oven reaches 225°F. Stir every 20 minutes or so to make sure the liquid doesn't scorch. Slice and serve.

If you wish, you can use a meat thermometer to determine when the roast is done. The internal temperature should read 165°F.

4 SERVINGS

1 (1 ½ - to 2-pound) pork loin roast

3 quarts whole milk

6 cloves garlic

3 sprigs fresh rosemary

1 teaspoon salt

½ teaspoon ground white pepper

Stinco d'Agnello Brasato
Lamb Shank Braised with Red Wine and Capers

Lamb shanks fare amazingly well with slow cooking techniques like braising and marry perfectly with the strong flavors of capers and anchovies.

2 SERVINGS

2 tablespoons olive oil

2 (10- to 12-ounce) lamb shanks

4 anchovy fillets

1 tablespoon dried sage

1 medium onion, chopped (about 1 cup)

8 cloves garlic, chopped

1 (28-ounce) can peeled, crushed tomatoes

1 cup red wine*

1 bay leaf

½ teaspoon salt

½ teaspoon freshly ground black pepper

3 tablespoons capers, rinsed and drained

Use either a zinfandel or a classic Piedmontese red like Nebbiolo.

Heat the oil in a heavy pan over medium heat. Brown the lamb shanks turning them frequently to color as much surface as you can. Remove the lamb and lower the heat.

Add the anchovies, sage, onion, and garlic. Cook, stirring, until the anchovies break down and the onions have begun to turn translucent. Add the tomatoes, wine, bay leaf, salt, and pepper, and bring the mixture to a boil for 1 minute. Reduce the heat and return the lamb shanks to the pot. Let them simmer for 1 hour, stirring occasionally. Mix in the capers and simmer for about 1 more hour. The dish is ready when the meat is fork tender.

Brasato al Vino Rosso
Beef Cooked in Red Wine

4 SERVINGS

In a place where great wine flows like water and beef is celebrated, here's a dish that combines them to great advantage.

¹/₄ **cup butter**

2 tablespoons olive oil

1 boneless eye round, rump roast, or brisket (about 5 pounds)

1 medium onion, chopped (about 1 cup)

2 large stalks celery, chopped (about 1 cup)

1 large red bell pepper, chopped (about 1 cup)

2 medium carrots, peeled and chopped (about 1 cup)

4 cloves garlic, chopped

2 sprigs fresh rosemary

2 bay leaves

2 fresh sage leaves

3 whole cloves

1 cinnamon stick

5 juniper berries

1 ¹/₂ teaspoons salt

1 ¹/₂ teaspoons freshly ground black pepper

1 bottle dry red wine*

1 cup beef or vegetable broth

Melt the butter with the olive oil in a Dutch oven over medium heat and brown the meat on all sides. Remove it from the pan and set aside. Place the onion, celery, bell pepper, carrot, garlic, rosemary, bay leaves, sage, cloves, cinnamon stick, and juniper berries in the pan, and cook, stirring, until the onions start to brown. Add the salt, pepper, wine, and broth, and bring to a boil for 1 minute. Return the meat to the Dutch oven and reduce the heat to medium-low. Simmer, covered, for 3 hours, turning the meat every 30 minutes. The last few times you turn it you'll have to be very careful; the roast will fall apart easily. When the meat is fork tender, remove it from the Dutch oven and keep it warm.

Discard the cinnamon stick and puree the remaining liquid and vegetables with either a food processor or an immersion blender.

To serve, place slices of meat on a plate and ladle the sauce over it. Don't throw away the sauce once the meat is gone! It's great on boiled potatoes, polenta, or pasta.

*You want a good, solid red here. Barolo, Barbaresco, and Barbera are the local choices, but maybe far too expensive for most of us to use this way. Any good cabernet sauvignon or zinfandel will do the job well.

Sacoccia
Boneless Stuffed Breast of Veal

This is a roast with a surprise inside. Some recipes omit the hard-boiled eggs but Maria's mother put them in so that when it's sliced open, there's the visual appeal of the orange yolk and brilliant white.

6 SERVINGS

¼ cup olive oil

½ pound ground pork

2 teaspoons salt

1 teaspoon freshly ground black pepper

5 scallions, finely chopped (1 cup)

2 ounces salami, chopped

2 cloves garlic, finely chopped

1 cup finely chopped fresh Italian parsley

5 fresh sage leaves, finely chopped

1 teaspoon chopped fresh thyme

1 teaspoon chopped fresh marjoram

1 teaspoon chopped fresh mint

2 eggs, lightly beaten

2 hard-boiled eggs, shelled

1 boneless breast of veal (about 2 pounds)*

2 cups beef broth

1 cup dry white wine

Ask the butcher to cut a pocket for stuffing.

Heat 2 tablespoons of the oil in a large skillet Add the ground pork, 1 teaspoon of the salt, and ½ teaspoon of the pepper. Add the scallions and sauté stirring until the meat is well browned. Transfer this mixture to a large bowl and let it cool. Add the salami, garlic, parsley, sage, thyme, marjoram, mint, 2 beaten eggs, the remaining salt and pepper to the pork and mix well.

Loosely stuff about half of the pork mixture into the pocket of the veal breast, then tuck in the hard-boiled eggs. Add the remaining stuffing to the pocket, but do not overstuff it—remember, the stuffing will expand— and tie the roast closed with kitchen twine.

In a large Dutch oven, heat in the remaining 2 tablespoons of oil over medium heat and brown the stuffed meat. Turn it several times to make sure it's cooked evenly. Add the broth and wine to the pot and lower the heat to a simmer. Cover the pot and cook for 90 minutes, turning the meat every 15 minutes so it cooks evenly.

Serve the roast in slices to show off the stuffing.

Arrosto di Vitello
Veal Roast

This stovetop method of dry cooking a veal roast dates back to the time when people didn't have home ovens. It isn't exactly dry roasting, but it's not braising either.

4 SERVINGS

3 tablespoons olive oil

1 (2-pound) veal roast

4 cloves garlic

1 sprig fresh rosemary

2 teaspoons salt

1 cup beef broth

1 cup white wine

Heat the oil in a heavy pan over medium heat and brown the roast with the garlic and rosemary. Turn the meat frequently to make sure that the entire surface browns evenly. Sprinkle the salt on the roast and cook over medium-low heat, covered, for 1 hour.

While the roast is cooking, drizzle tablespoons of broth and wine over the meat every few minutes to make sure it doesn't burn. The roast is ready when an instant-read meat thermometer shows a temperature of 160°F. Remove it from the pan, place on a serving platter and let rest for 10 minutes before slicing and serving.

Bollito Misto
Mixed Boiled Meats

10 TO 12 SERVINGS

3 tablespoons salt

1 large onion, quartered

3 carrots, peeled and cut
into large chunks

3 stalks celery,
cut into large chunks

1/2 cup chopped fresh parsley

1 sprig fresh rosemary

1/2 stewing hen
(about 1 1/2 to 2 pounds)

1 1/2 to 2 pounds chuck roast

1 1/2 to 2 pounds veal breast

1 to 1 1/2 pounds oxtail,
cut into 2-inch pieces

1 beef tongue
(about 1 1/2 to 2 pounds)

1 cotechino sausage
(about 12 ounces)

Bollito Misto is a big dish. It's perfect for groups, parties, and other special events. It's big in other ways, too: you'll need at least a couple of large pots—holding twelve and sixteen quarts—to prepare it and, when you do, you'll make an impression that will be ... well, big.

To some people, this dish conjures up images of another time—the idle rich of the nineteenth century away in their hilltop castles. It's a dish from a different era that has escaped the notice of most modern-day cooks. In Piemonte today, it is most often eaten at a country restaurant, and isn't easy to find.

In Maria's family, a reduced version of this dish (using half the red meat and leaving out the hen) was eaten every week during the winter months. It was a practical way of cooking several meals at once, since leftovers would be reused in many different ways: In the following days, the beef reappeared chopped in a salad dressed simply with olive oil and red wine vinegar. Potatoes were added to the boiled onion and carrot, and made into a winter vegetable medley. The meat broth was used for risotto at lunch or in soups at dinner.

Bring 8 quarts of water to a boil in a 12-quart stock pot. Add the salt, onion, carrots, celery, parsley, and rosemary, and stir well. Add the chicken and return the mixture to a boil. Add the chuck roast, veal breast, oxtail, and tongue. Return to a boil for 1 minute, then reduce the heat to a simmer

After 90 minutes, remove the chicken and let the rest of the meat simmer for 2 more hours, skimming the foam from the surface of the cooking liquid as needed. Return the chicken to the cooking liquid and cook 10 more minutes.

With a fork, pierce the cotechino, put it another pot filled with cold water to cover, bring to a boil, and cook for 1 hour.

Slice all the meats and serve hot on a serving platter. Serve with at least two of the traditional accompanying sauces (recipes follow) and try to make sure that everybody gets a taste of each item.

Note: Traditionally, this dish contained seven cuts of meat. However, the seven that were used were never universally agreed upon. Older recipes almost certainly called for veal heads (or at least some tissue from the veal skull, called *testina*) and hearts. Don't be afraid to experiment if you can obtain these unusual cuts.

Bagnet Vert
Green Sauce

Bagnet Vert is a classic both in Piemonte and in Argentina, where a spicier variation is served with steaks and other grilled meats.

MAKES 2 CUPS

1 bunch chopped fresh parsley
(about 1 cup)

3 tablespoons capers,
rinsed and drained

4 salted anchovies,
boned and rinsed

2 cloves garlic

2 hard-boiled egg yolks

1 cup stale bread cubes
(crusts removed)

1 cup extra-virgin olive oil

½ cup red wine vinegar

Combine the parsley, capers, anchovies, garlic, egg yolks, bread, oil, and vinegar in a food processor, and puree until smooth. Pour into a nonreactive container and let stand for at least 1 hour at room temperature before serving, to let the flavors combine. Store in the refrigerator up to 2 weeks.

Bagnet Ross
Red Sauce

Bagnet Ross is more mellow than Bagnet Vert. It requires a bit of effort, but if you're going to do the Bollito Misto, this is an important component.

MAKES 2 CUPS

2 tablespoons olive oil

1 medium onion, coarsely chopped (about 1 cup)

1 (28-ounce) can peeled, crushed tomatoes

red and/or yellow bell peppers, cut into strips

1 stalk celery, chopped (1 cup)

1 teaspoon salt

1 teaspoon freshly ground black pepper

1 teaspoon red pepper flakes

Heat the oil over medium heat and sauté the onion until it is translucent. Add the peppers and celery, and cook, stirring, until the peppers are fork tender. Add the tomatoes, salt, ground pepper, and chili flakes and simmer, stirring occasionally, until the liquid has reduced by about half. Allow the sauce to cool, then pour it into a food processor and puree. Serve warm.

Salsa Dell'Uomo Povero
Poor Man's Sauce

A simple onion and wine sauce.

MAKES 1 CUP

1 tablespoon olive oil

1 medium onion, chopped
(about 1 cup)

3 large shallots, chopped
(about ½ cup)

3 scallions, chopped
(about ¼ cup)

3 cloves garlic

1 cup dry red wine

¼ cup beef broth

¼ teaspoon salt

In a large saucepan, heat the oil over medium heat. Add the onion, shallots, scallions and garlic until the onions are golden. Add the wine, broth, and salt, increase the heat to high, and bring the mixture to a boil. Boil for 1 minute and then reduce the heat to medium-low. Simmer, uncovered, stirring occasionally, until the liquid has reduced by half. Remove from the heat. Puree the mixture in a blender or food processor so that you have a thick sauce.

Saosa d'Avije
Honey Sauce

If you thought the combination of honey and mustard were modern and/or American, you're in for a surprise with this simple sauce.

MAKES 1 1/2 CUPS

1 tablespoon French hot mustard

1 tablespoon white wine vinegar

½ cup beef broth

½ cup honey

1 ½ ounces chopped walnuts (about ½ cup)

In a small bowl, use a fork to beat the mustard, vinegar, and 1 tablespoon of the warm broth into a smooth liquid.

Warm the honey in a double boiler, remove from the heat and stir in the walnuts. Immediately add the mustard mixture and add the remaining broth as needed to produce a sauce.

Let stand for at least 1 hour before serving, so the flavors can combine. At the table, provide a mixing spoon to make sure that the walnuts don't settle to the bottom.

Finanziera all'Albese

Stewed Riches

½ pound ground veal

1 cup all-purpose flour

½ pound beef or veal marrow

½ pound calves' brains

½ pound veal sweetbreads

¼ pound chicken livers

¼ pound cockscombs

¼ cup butter

½ pound veal cutlet, cut into 1/2-inch strips

1 cup dry red wine

2 cups chicken broth

1 tablespoon olive oil

1 cup fresh green peas

½ cup mushrooms marinated in oil*

1 tablespoon red wine vinegar

2 tablespoons dry marsala wine

2 teaspoons salt

Use any oil marinated mushrooms you can find, but porcini are best. Look for them at gourmet, Italian, or Polish markets.

Depending on how adventurous you are, this is a stew of either luxurious or horrifying ingredients. We won't try to convince the squeamish, but for those who appreciate offal, this is truly a glorious dish. Because of its intense flavor, nowadays it is often served as an appetizer. Different variations of this dish exist; this version from Langhe uses peas for a pleasing green touch. It's said that the secret of success is to cook each ingredient separately.

Form the ground veal into ¾-inch meatballs and dredge in the flour. Cut the marrow, brains, sweetbreads, chicken livers, and cockscombs into bite-size cubes, dredge in flour, and keep separate by type.

In a pan large enough to hold all the ingredients, melt 1 tablespoon of the butter and brown the veal cutlet strips. When the edges of the meat are golden, lower the heat to low and add 2 tablespoons of the broth and 1 tablespoon of wine.

In a separate pan, melt another ½ tablespoon of the butter and cook the veal meatballs over low heat. Add the meatballs to the pan with the veal.

Heat ½ tablespoon of the butter over medium heat in the same pan used to cook the meatballs and sauté the floured marrow pieces. When they are golden, stir them into the main pan along with 2 tablespoons of the broth and 1 tablespoon of wine.

Sauté the brains, sweetbreads, livers, and cockscombs separately in ½ tablespoon of butter each, and transfer to the big pot along with 2 tablespoons of broth and 1 tablespoon of wine.

Heat the olive oil in a small saucepan and cook the peas with the remaining ¼ cup of broth until tender. Add the peas and to the main pot.

Sauté the mushrooms in their own oil until they begin to brown, and transfer them to the main pot.

At this point, the sauce in the main pot should have the consistency of a gravy. Add the vinegar and marsala, raise the heat to medium and stir to combine all the ingredients—about 2 minutes.

Serve immediately.

Trippa con Patate e Fagioli
Stewed Tripe with Potatoes and Beans

4 SERVINGS

2 tablespoons olive oil

1 tablespoon lard

4 ounces pancetta, minced

½ pound boneless pork loin, cut into ¾-inch cubes

1 tablespoon dried sage

1 teaspoon dried thyme

1 teaspoon dried oregano

1 pound tripe, cut into 1-inch strips*

2 bay leaves

1 cup marsala wine

2 Yukon gold potatoes, peeled and cubed (about 2 cups)

1 cup canned crushed tomatoes

1 (15 ½-ounce) can Roman beans, drained and rinsed

If you're using honeycomb tripe (the most common kind) you'll need to simmer it in salted water for 2 to 3 hours before adding it. You can also use omasum (often called "bible tripe"), which is found in Asian grocery stores; it cooks quickly and can be incorporated as is.

This dish is a treat for organ meat fans. It combines three classic stewing ingredients in one dish: tripe, potatoes, and beans.

Heat the oil in a large, heavy pot and sauté the lard, pancetta, pork loin, sage, thyme, and oregano until the pancetta and pork loin begin to brown. Add the tripe and make sure it's thoroughly coated with the lard mixture. Add 2 cups of water, the bay leaves and marsala, raise the heat to high, and bring the mixture to a boil for 1 minute. Reduce the heat to a simmer and cook for 1 hour, stirring occasionally. Then add the potatoes, tomatoes, and beans. Simmer for 1 more hour. The dish is ready when the potatoes are fork tender.

Verdure

[V E G E T A B L E S]

Vegetables are an important part of the Piedmontese diet. They're sold in every market and find their way into an astounding array of dishes. On a typical weekday, Maria's parents usually had some young celery stalks or few slices of tomato and pepper drizzled with olive oil and vinegar as an antipasto.

Apart from antipasti, dishes that feature vegetables on their own are rare, although they are important in soups, risottos, pasta sauces, and stews. There are a few vegetable dishes that are important however, and we present them here. Many of the vegetables called for are uncommon in the United States; for example, cardoons are almost unheard of, and turnips though available, are almost unknown to Americans as an element of Italian cooking. Don't be afraid to give these strangers a try, they bring interesting new tastes to the table.

Peperonata
Sautéed Bell Peppers

6 SERVINGS

2 tablespoons olive oil

1 medium onion, sliced

2 cloves garlic, chopped

3 medium yellow peppers, cut into
$\frac{1}{2}$-inch-wide strips

3 medium red peppers, cut into
$\frac{1}{2}$-inch-wide strips

1 sprig fresh rosemary

2 cups, crushed tomatoes*

$\frac{1}{4}$ cup loosely packed
fresh basil leaves

1 teaspoon salt

$\frac{1}{2}$ teaspoon freshly ground
black pepper

*Use either canned, peeled, crushed
tomatoes or the Italian product
known as pelati.

Not far from Cuneo, the town of Carmagnola is known for its red and yellow bell peppers. These find their way into appetizers, meat dishes and sauces on a regular basis, but during peak season, they also become the centerpiece of this popular vegetable side dish.

Heat the olive oil in a skillet over medium heat. Add the onion and cook, stirring, until translucent. Add the garlic and cook until the onion begins to turn golden—about 20 minutes. Mix in the peppers and rosemary, and cook until the peppers begin to soften. Add the tomato, basil, salt, and pepper, and simmer, uncovered, stirring occasionally, until the liquid has reduced by about one-third and the flavors have combined.

Serve warm as a side dish, or warm or cold as an appetizer.

Cardi con Besciamella

Cardoons in White Sauce

4 SERVINGS

1 head cardoons (about 2 pounds), cleaned and cut into 3-inch sections

1 teaspoon salt

¼ cup Parmesan cheese, grated

WHITE SAUCE (BESCIAMELLA):

¼ teaspoon salt

2 cups milk

3 tablespoons butter

2 tablespoons all-purpose flour

½ teaspoon freshly grated nutmeg

Cardoons? Does anybody even know what they are? They look like celery and taste a bit like artichokes. Cardoons are a winter vegetable, in season from October to December; in the cold climate of Piemonte, that's a valuable asset.

Preheat the oven to 325°F. Grease a 9 x 13-inch baking dish.

Sprinkle the cardoons with the salt and steam over medium heat until fork tender, about 45 minutes.

For the white sauce: Warm the milk in a saucepan over very low heat; keep warm. Melt the butter in a skillet over medium-low heat and mix in the flour, using a wooden spoon or whisk. Cook, stirring, for 3 more minutes, or until the raw flour taste is gone. Mix in the warm milk a few drops at a time and keep stirring until each addition of milk is absorbed and all the lumps are gone. Stir in the nutmeg.

Place the cardoon pieces in the prepared pan and cover them with the white sauce. Sprinkle with the cheese and bake for about 5 minutes. Serve warm.

Carote Fritte
Fried Carrots

Carote Fritte are among the most commonly served vegetables during the winter months and are ideal companions to all kinds of Piedmontese meat dishes. Even though the Italian name implies that the carrots are fried, they're really sautéed in a skillet. For most cooks, the big question when cooking vegetables this way is, "Butter or olive oil?" This recipe calls for both but, like many Italians, you can reduce the butter and increase the olive oil if you wish.

4 SERVINGS

3 tablespoons olive oil

1 tablespoon butter

2 cloves garlic

1 bay leaf

1 sprig fresh rosemary

5 medium carrots, peeled and thinly sliced

1 teaspoon salt

Heat the oil and melt the butter in a skillet over medium heat. Add the garlic, bay leaf and rosemary and cook, stirring, until the garlic begins to turn translucent. Add the carrots, sprinkle with the salt and cook, stirring occasionally, until they are fork tender—about 15 minutes. If they dry out and begin to scorch, add 3 tablespoons of water to the pan. Serve warm.

Cavolfiore in Salsa Piccante
Cauliflower in Spicy Sauce

Piedmontese food isn't spicy in the sense that Thai food is, or even food from Amalfi or other places in southern Italy, but by local standards this dish is pretty strongly flavored.

4 SERVINGS

1 tablespoon salt

1 head cauliflower
(1 ¼ to 2 pounds)

6 tablespoons butter

4 salted anchovies,
rinsed and boned

1 bunch fresh Italian parsley,
chopped (about 1 cup)

3 tablespoons lemon juice

Bring 4 quarts of water to a boil with the salt. Add the cauliflower, and reduce the heat to medium. Simmer, covered for 15 minutes, or until it is fork tender. Drain and set aside.

Melt the butter in a separate saucepan over medium-low heat, add the anchovies and parsley and cook, stirring, until the anchovies have broken down and the parsley has completely wilted.

Cut the cooked cauliflower into bite-size pieces and place them in a serving bowl. Pour the butter sauce and lemon juice over them and toss well. Serve warm.

Finocchi con Burro e Noce Moscato
Fennel with Butter and Nutmeg

4 SERVINGS

1 tablespoon plus 1 teaspoon salt

3 bulbs fennel, sliced*

2 tablespoons butter

1/2 teaspoon freshly grated nutmeg

3 tablespoons grated Parmesan cheese

To slice the fennel, first cut off the base, stem and leaves and then cut the remaining bulb in half by slicing it lengthwise from top to bottom. Then slice it against the grain into 1/4-inch strips.

Fennel is that aromatic vegetable that looks sort of like celery and has a distinct licorice scent and flavor. In addition to being one of the vegetables dipped in Bagna Cauda (page 26) and eaten raw in salads, fennel is prepared with butter and cheese, as are many vegetables for the Piedmontese table.

Bring 4 quarts of water to a boil with 1 tablespoon of the salt. Add the fennel and reduce the heat to medium. Simmer, covered, for 5 minutes, or until the slices have started to soften. Drain and set aside.

Melt the butter in a large skillet over medium-low heat, stir in the fennel, and sprinkle with the remaining 1 teaspoon of salt. Cook, stirring, for 3 minutes, then cover the pan and cook for another 10 minutes, stirring occasionally. If the fennel starts to dry out, add a few tablespoons of water. When the fennel is fork tender, sprinkle with the nutmeg and Parmesan, and serve immediately.

Spinaci al Burro
Sautéed Spinach

4 SERVINGS

1 tablespoon salt

2 pounds fresh spinach, thoroughly rinsed clean of sand or 1 (10-once) package frozen spinach, thawed

3 tablespoons butter

3 cloves garlic, chopped

This is the basic Piedmontese recipe for leafy greens. Spinach is most common, but this dish is also prepared with Swiss chard and other vegetables. In Piemonte, most people put grated Parmesan cheese on top of almost everything and this dish is be no exception—serve it that way for a pleasant surprise.

In a large pot, bring 4 quarts of water a boil with the salt. Add the spinach, stir, and reduce the heat to medium. When the leaves are bright green and fully wilted— about 3 minutes—drain thoroughly, and let cool. Squeeze the spinach with your hands to remove as much moisture as possible.

Melt the butter in a skillet over medium-low heat and add the garlic. Cook, stirring, until it begins to turn translucent—about 5 minutes—and then add the spinach. Keep cooking until all the spinach is warm and coated with the butter and the garlic is evenly distributed. Serve immediately.

Rape con Salsiccia
Turnips with Sausage

*With the sausage permeating the entire dish, this is an intensely flavorful way to cook turnips. In Piemonte, this would be made with **salsiccia di Bra**, but any mild pork or lamb sausage will do a fine job.*

4 SERVINGS

1 ¼ teaspoons salt

1 ½ pounds turnips, peeled and sliced

3 tablespoons butter

½ teaspoon freshly ground black pepper

1 pound sweet pork sausage, cut into 1 inch long pieces

Bring 4 quarts of water to a boil with the salt. Add the turnips, reduce the heat to medium and simmer for 5 minutes. Remove the turnips from the pot and rinse them under cold water.

Melt the butter in a large skillet over medium-low heat and stir in the turnips until they are well coated with butter and warmed through. Add the pepper and sausage and continue cooking, stirring occasionally, until the meat is cooked through. Serve warm.

Ratatuja
Vegetable Stew

4 SERVINGS

2 tablespoons olive oil

6 salted anchovies, rinsed and boned

1 bay leaf

Yukon Gold potatoes, cubed (about 2 cups)

1 medium onion, chopped (about 1 cup)

2 celery stalk, chopped (about 1 cup)

1 large red or yellow bell pepper, cut into strips

2 medium carrots, peeled and chopped (about 1 cup)

1 medium eggplant, cubed (about 2 cups)

1 medium zucchini, sliced

1 cup canned peeled, crushed tomatoes

3 cloves garlic

1/4 cup loosely packed fresh basil

1/2 cup chopped fresh Italian parsley

6 fresh sage leaves

1/4 cup red wine vinegar

2 tablespoons capers, rinsed and drained

Ratatouille, the French version of this dish from neighboring Provence is well known in the United States, but this one—garnished with capers, raw garlic, anchovies, and herbs—is solidly on Piedmontese turf.

Heat the oil in a large pot over medium heat and stir in 2 of the anchovies. When they break down, add the bay leaf, potatoes, onion, celery, pepper, and carrot. Cook, stirring, until the onions and potatoes brown—about 30 minutes. Mix in the eggplant, zucchini, and tomato, and simmer, uncovered, for 45 minutes more, until all the vegetables are fork tender and the liquid has reduced into a thick sauce.

Mince the remaining 4 anchovies, garlic, basil, parsley, and sage and combine with the vinegar and capers.

To serve, put the cooked vegetables on individual plates and spoon the anchovy mixture on top.

Dolci

[SWEETS & DESSERTS]

Whether at the end of a great meal, or the high point of a visit to a big city café, sweets, desserts, and baked goods are an important part of Piedmontese life. A tray of cookies says "hello" when you're visiting friends, a flan marks the end of a monumental meal at the dining room table, and a beautiful pastry frames your memory of a shopping trip in town.

As always, the area's history as a major trading center and dairy producer sets the ingredient list: nuts, eggs, cream, fruit, butter, and wine are all from the region; and cocoa and sugar were both important trade items. Combined in the Piedmontese way, they create a special palette of sweets.

When you're in town, you'll quickly find out that each pastry shop has its own specialty—one could have a remarkable cookie, another might offer a distinctive cake. All are different than what people prepare at home, where cooked fruits, custards, and relatively simple baked goods are commonly served.

Paste di Meliga
Cornmeal Cookies

*Finely ground yellow cornmeal (**meliga**) gives these cookies a pleasant, sunny color. Serve them at the end of a meal with a glass of Barolo and some Zabaione (page 130) for dipping. They are also good alone or with fruit salad.*

18 COOKIES

1 ½ cups finely ground yellow cornmeal

¾ cup all-purpose flour

1 cup confectioner's sugar

4 tablespoons butter

2 egg yolks, lightly beaten

1 teaspoon grated lemon peel

¼ teaspoon salt

Preheat the oven to 325°F. Grease and flour a baking sheet.

In a bowl combine the cornmeal, flour, sugar, butter, egg yolks, lemon peel, and salt. With your hands, form tablespoons of the dough into balls. Put them on the baking sheet, pressing them flat with your hands. With a knife, trace a cross on the surface of each cookie. Bake for 20 minutes, or until golden brown.

Baci di Dama

Dame's Kisses

These cookies are found in pastry shops and bakeries everywhere in Piemonte. Their name comes from their shape: two bisected spheres of buttery dough bound together with a kiss of melted chocolate.

72 COOKIES

10 ounces hazelnuts or almonds, toasted, peeled, and finely chopped (about 2 ¼ cups)

2 ¼ cups all-purpose flour

1 ½ cup sugar

1 cup butter, warmed at room temperature

1 teaspoon baking powder

2 eggs

3 ounces unsweetened chocolate

Preheat the oven to 325°F. Line a baking sheet with parchment paper.

Combine the nuts, flour, sugar, butter, baking powder, and eggs and mix well with an electric mixer. You should have a thick dough. Using ¾-inch pieces of dough, form the dough into half-spheres (you should get about 40 to 50) and place them on the prepared baking sheet. Bake for 20 minutes. Set aside to cool.

In the meantime, melt the chocolate in a double boiler over low heat, stirring constantly. Dip the flat side of each half-sphere in the melted chocolate and press two together to form a full sphere with the chocolate in the middle. Let them cool and serve.

Store in a cool place so the chocolate doesn't melt.

d

Buying Hazelnuts

You will not be able to find the round Langhe hazelnut outside Italy. However, we have been quite satisfied with other Mediterranean varieties. (Look for them in Middle Eastern groceries.) Try to buy hazelnuts that are as fresh as possible; stores where they are kept refrigerated are best.

Hazelnuts—sometimes called filberts—are sold in at least three different ways: in the shells; shelled, with the dark brown skin still on; and blanched with both the skin and shell removed. Because of the work involved, it's tempting to buy skinned hazelnuts, but we found them disappointing. As they can be difficult to shell, however, we recommend buying hazelnuts with shells removed and skins still on.

Removing the skins is not that difficult, just time consuming.

Preheat the oven at a pan in the 350°F. Spread the hazelnuts on a baking sheet and toast them in the oven for 30 minutes. Remove the pan from the oven and gather batches of the nuts in a kitchen towel. Rub them together in the towel. The skins should peel off easily. Don't worry if the hazelnuts are not completely skinless. The toasted skin will give a darker color and extra fiber to your dish, but that small bit won't affect flavor.

Brutti ma Buoni

Hazelnut Cookies

"Ugly but good" is what the name means and they're another simple, traditional cookie with those Piedmontese baking basics: hazelnuts and eggs.

24 COOKIES

10 ounces hazelnuts, toasted and peeled

1 ½ cups sugar

4 egg whites

½ teaspoon salt

½ teaspoon vanilla extract

Preheat the oven to 325°F. Lay a piece of parchment paper on a baking sheet.

Finely grind the hazelnuts in a food processor and combine with the sugar. Beat the egg whites with the salt until stiff peaks form. Carefully fold the egg whites into the hazelnut mixture and add the vanilla.

Spoon heaping tablespoons of the batter on the prepared baking sheet. Leave a space the size of the each cookie in between. The dough will form irregular blobs.

Bake for 35 minutes, then cool for 15 minutes on the pan. They'll keep for several weeks in an airtight container.

Variation: Substitute almonds for hazelnuts.

d

Coppette
Nut and Honey Wafers

A traditional farmer's dessert that was made for New Year's day using ingredients that can be foraged from Piemonte's forests. The wafers—the same one's used by priests at communion—were among the few things that people a century ago would buy commercially.

36 WAFERS

12 ounces walnuts, chopped (about 2 ½ cups)

2 cups honey

3 sheets wafer paper*, cut into 2-inch squares

*Large sheets of a communion wafer-like material are used in cake decorating and available from baking supplies shops.

Mix the walnuts and honey in a saucepan over low heat, stirring for 5 minutes. Remove from heat. Lay half of the wafers on a flat surface and pour the honey mixture over them, then cover with the remaining wafers. Put a layer of parchment paper over the finished wafers and weigh them down - you can use bags of dry beans. Set aside for 3 of hours, then serve.

Palline di Castagne e Amaretti
Chestnut Balls

Hazelnuts aren't the only nuts in the Piedmontese kitchen; chestnuts have traditionally also played an important role. You'll find them in sauces, stuffings, and in desserts like these.

24 BALLS

1 bay leaf

1 tablespoon salt

10 ounces fresh chestnuts, in their shells

2 tablespoons butter, at room temperature

2 tablespoons unsweetened cocoa

2 ounces hard amaretti cookies, crushed (about 1 cup)

2 tablespoons rum

½ cup confectioner's sugar

Bring 4 cups of water to a boil with the bay leaves and salt. Cut a slit in the shell of each chestnut; this will keep them from bursting and make them easier to peel. Add the chestnuts to the water, reduce the heat to a simmer, and cook for 45 minutes. Remove the chestnuts from the water and peel them while they're still warm. Put them in a food processor with the butter, cocoa, and amaretti crumbs. Mix until the mixture is completely blended into a thick dough. Use a tablespoon of dough to form a ball and roll it in the confectioner's sugar. Set the finished balls on a platter and chill. Serve cold.

Bugie
Fried Dough for Carnevale

*Crunchier than zeppole their well-known southern cousin, this fried sweet dough is just one of the many versions of the ancient Roman frictilia. **Bugie** means "lies" in English and they are traditionally eaten at **Carnevale**, when one can tell a lie without repercussions, especially if they're as small and simple as these sweets are. Grappa gives them a distinctive pungency.*

Combine the flour, eggs, butter, grappa, and marsala with an electric mixer. Remove from the mixer and knead on a floured surface for about 5 minutes, or until the dough becomes elastic. Wrap in plastic wrap and let rest for 1 hour at room temperature.

Roll the dough out on a flat, floured surface until it's about ⅛ inch thick. Using a fluted pastry wheel, cut 4 x 2-inch rectangles or triangles. Cover with a towel to prevent them from drying out.

Heat the oil in heavy pot to 350°F. Gently lower several pieces of dough into the hot oil and fry until golden brown. Make sure the oil returns to the correct temperature before adding another batch of dough. Drain the cookies on a rack or paper towels. When they are slightly cooled, sprinkle with the confectioner's sugar.

36 PIECES

2 ¼ cups all-purpose flour

2 eggs

1/4 cup butter, at room temperature

¼ cup grappa*

2 tablespoons marsala wine

8 cups peanut oil

2 tablespoons confectioner's sugar

*Don't use one of those fancy grappas, they'll be too mild. Instead find a typical and moderately priced bottle. It's also great in espresso.

Gianduiotto
Chocolate Almond Icebox Cake

4 SERVINGS

2 eggs, lightly beaten or 3 ounces pasteurized egg whites

1 cup sugar

1 cup unsweetened cocoa

1 stick butter

3 tablespoons ground, toasted almonds

4 ounces hard amaretti cookies, crushed (about 2 cups)

¼ cup heavy cream, whipped

*Turin loves **Gianduiotti**, the wedge-shaped hazelnut chocolates wrapped in golden tin foil that have become a symbol of the city. They were first created in 1865 by Caffarel, a chocolatier, who named them after **Gianduia**, Turin's Carnival mask. **Gianduiotti** quickly became popular and were considered revolutionary for their unusual base (a mixture of hazelnut and chocolate), their wedge shape, and for being the first wrapped chocolates. Due to their popularity, the name **gianduiotto** is often used to refer to many sweet concoctions that mix nuts and chocolate. This icebox cake combining almonds with chocolate is just one example.*

In a bowl, beat the eggs and sugar until foamy. Stir in the cocoa, making sure there are no lumps.

Cut the butter into small pieces, put it in a cup, and gently warm it by holding it over a steaming pot—the butter should be liquid and at room temperature. Whisk the butter into the sugar mixture until all the ingredients are combined into a thick batter. Fold in almond and amaretti crumbs just until combined.

Line an 8 ½ x 4 ½ -inch loaf pan with waxed paper and pour in the mixture. Put the loaf pan in the refrigerator and chill for 3 to 4 hours, until set. When you are ready to serve it, turn it out onto a platter and garnish with the whipped cream. Serve cold and store in the refrigerator.

Torta di Nocciole
Hazelnut Cake

Hazelnuts are used frequently in Piedmontese sweets. They come in several, subtly different varieties, with the round ones from Langhe being most prized. This cake, from the home of those round nuts, is found in bakeries, restaurants, and homes—often under a sweet sauce like Zabaione (page 130). This cake is also frequently paired with wine. Dessert wines like Moscato or even strong reds like Barolo and Barbaresco work very well.

6 SERVINGS

2 egg yolks

⅓ cup sugar

½ cup butter, at room temperature

1 teaspoon grated lemon peel

½ cup all-purpose flour

1 teaspoon baking powder

1 teaspoon vanilla extract

8 ounces hazelnuts, toasted, peeled, and finely chopped (about 2 cups)

Preheat the oven to 350°F. Grease and flour a 9-inch pie or round cake pan.

Combine the egg yolks and sugar, and beat with an electric mixer until the sugar is fully dissolved and the mixture is pale yellow. Mix in the butter, lemon peel, flour, baking powder, vanilla, and hazelnuts, until they form a wet dough. Place the dough in the prepared pan. Bake for 40 minutes, cool, and serve at room temperature.

Zuppa Inglese
Ladyfinger Cake

Zuppa Inglese means "English Soup," but this cake is neither English nor a soup. Historically, it comes from Piemonte, but today you can find it almost anywhere in Italy. Along with **Bonet** (page 127), this was a dessert that never failed to show up at the end of Sunday lunches during Maria's childhood.

6 SERVINGS

FOR THE EGG CUSTARD

2 egg yolks

2 tablespoons sugar

1 ½ teaspoons all-purpose flour

½ cup heavy cream

½ cups milk

FOR THE CHOCOLATE CREAM:

2 egg yolks

2 tablespoons sugar

1 ½ teaspoons all-purpose flour

2 tablespoons unsweetened cocoa

1 cup milk

4 ounces semisweet or bittersweet chocolate, grated

1 ½ cups espresso, at room temperature

7 ounces ladyfinger cookies (about 20)

To prepare the custard, beat the egg yolks with the sugar until foamy, and then stir in the flour. Then, add the cream and milk. Slowly bring the mixture to a rapid simmer and stir constantly. Simmer for 1 minute, remove from the heat, and set aside.

In another saucepan, make the chocolate cream by beating the egg yolks and the sugar until foamy. Stir in the flour and the cocoa. Then add the milk and bring the mixture to a rapid simmer while stirring constantly. Simmer for 1 minute, then remove it from the heat and mix in the grated chocolate. Stir until the chocolate is completely melted and evenly combined with the other ingredients.

Moisten the ladyfingers with the espresso and place a layer of them in a 2 quart baking dish—this forms the base of the cake. Cover them with a layer of egg custard. Then place a second layer of coffee-moistened ladyfingers and cover them with chocolate cream.

Refrigerate for at least 2 hours and serve cold.

Torta Monferrina di Zucca e Mele
Pumpkin and Apple Cake

*This cake is from Monferrato, the hilly area surrounding Asti. It is a simple, rustic cake that you can prepare for a Piedmontese-style Halloween celebration called **Festa della Zucca** in Italian.*

6 SERVINGS

¼ cup raisins

6 dried figs, chopped (½ cup)

½ cup sweet marsala wine

3 cups diced pumpkin (about 1 pound)

4 apples, peeled and diced (about 2 cups)

1 cup whole milk

1 cup sugar

2 eggs, lightly beaten

4 ounces unsweetened chocolate

2 ounces bittersweet chocolate

1 ounce hard amaretti cookies, crushed (about ½ cup)

½ teaspoon lemon peel

½ teaspoon vanilla extract

3 tablespoons rum

Preheat the oven to 275°F. Grease a 9-inch square pan.

Soak the raisins and figs in the marsala for 30 minutes, drain, and set aside.

Combine the pumpkin, apples, milk, and sugar in a large pot over low heat. Simmer, covered, stirring occasionally, until the pumpkin is fork tender. Mix in the eggs, both types of chocolate, amaretti crumbs, lemon peel, vanilla, rum, and soaked dried fruit.

Pour the batter into the prepared pan and level it with a spatula. Bake for 3 hours, until a toothpick inserted in the center comes out dry.

Bonet
Chocolate Flan

8 SERVINGS

5 eggs

5 tablespoons sugar

2 tablespoons unsweetened cocoa

2 ounces hard amaretti cookies, crushed (about 1 cup)

2 tablespoons rum

1 cup milk

1 recipe Basic Caramelized Sugar (page 132)

*Growing up, Maria often visited relatives in Carrù for Sunday lunch. Most of the time, the meal ended with **Bonet**, flan made with chocolate and amaretti, found everywhere in Langhe and Monferrato. **Bonet** works well in all seasons and, even though it could never be described as light, it goes down easily after a rich meal. The word **bonet** means "hat" and refers to the traditional round form of this dessert.*

Preheat the oven to 325°F.

Beat the eggs well in a large bowl or stand mixer and add the sugar, cocoa, amaretti crumbs, rum, and milk. Set aside.

Pour the caramelized sugar into a 9 x 5-inch loaf pan or caramelize the sugar directly in the pan. Tilt the pan to distribute the sugar as evenly as possible. Pour the flan into the pan, cover it with a lid or foil, and place it in a larger pan filled with 2 inches of water to form a bain-marie. Put it in the oven and bake for 40 minutes, or until a toothpick inserted in the center comes out clean. Cool in the refrigerator for at least 2 hours. Run a knife around the edges and unmold onto a platter. Serve chilled or at room temperature.

Bonet al Caffè
Espresso Flan

4 SERVINGS

6 eggs

¼ cup sugar

2 tablespoons unsweetened cocoa

½ ounce hard amaretti cookies, crushed (about ¼ cup)

1 tablespoon rum or Amaretto liqueur

1 teaspoon grated lemon peel

1 cup prepared espresso, at room temperature

1 cup heavy cream

1 recipe Basic Caramelized Sugar (page 133)

3 cups boiling water

With a rich espresso flavor, this is the perfect Piedmontese treat for coffee fanatics.

Preheat the oven at 325°F.

Beat the eggs in a blender or food processor until well blended and then add the sugar, cocoa, amaretti, rum, lemon peel, espresso, and cream. Make sure everything is well combined and there are no lumps.

Warm an 2-quart baking dish by filling it with hot water. Let sit for 1 minute, empty it, and wipe dry. Pour the caramelized sugar into the dish, tilting so it spreads evenly. Then pour in the flan and cover the dish with aluminum foil.

Fill a larger pan with 1 inch of water and place the pan with the flan in it to form a bain-marie. Bake for 60 minutes, a toothpick inserted in the center comes out clean.

Remove from the oven and let cool for at least 1 hour in the refrigerator.

To serve, run a knife around the edges and invert the dish onto a platter.

Budino delle Langhe
Panna Cotta

4 SERVINGS

1 envelope (1 tablespoon)
unflavored gelatin

½ cup whole milk

2 cups heavy cream

½ cup plus 1 tablespoons sugar

¼ teaspoon salt

½ teaspoon vanilla extract

¼ cup rum

Panna Cotta is a well-known dessert with deep roots in Piedmontese cuisine. Maria's mother—a native of Langhe—always called it **Budino delle Langhe** *("flan from Langhe"). She used* **colla di pesce**—*gelatin made from fish bones—to solidify it, but unflavored gelatin crystals will do the job.*

Sprinkle the gelatin over the milk and set aside until the gelatin is moist and translucent—about 4 minutes. Stir gently

Combine the cream, ⅛ cup plus 1 tablespoon of the sugar, and the salt in a saucepan and bring to a simmer. Add the gelatin mixture and remove from the heat. Mix in the vanilla and rum, and set aside.

Caramelize the remaining ⅛ cup of sugar (page 133). Divide the caramelized sugar between four (8-ounce) ramekins, making sure the sides are evenly coated. Pour in the panna cotta mixture and chill until set—about 3 hours.

For an elegant presentation, garnish each ramekin with sliced almonds and berries

Zabaione
Zabaglione

Zabaglione is found all over Italy, but most commonly in Piemonte. Of course, local cooks put their own stamp on the dish by using Moscato or Barolo wines instead of marsala.

4 SERVINGS

8 eggs yolks

1 cup sugar

1 cup Moscato wine

In Piemonte there's a legend about the origin of the name: The dish was supposedly created by a Franciscan brother, Pasquale Baylon, now patron saint of Turin's chefs. In local dialect, San Baylon would be pronounced "san Bajon." This was shortened to "sanbajon" and then morphed into the word we use today. In his confessional, Baylon advised women to prepare a mixture of eggs, sugar, and wine to restore their husband's strength. In fact, traditionally zabaglione wasn't considered a dessert, but rather a savory, restorative mid-afternoon snack for invalids. It was also what Maria's father advised his daughters to consume whenever they were under stress from their studies.

Nowadays Zabaione is eaten warm or cold. Serve it alone, with a few simple cookies (Paste di Meliga are a classic choice; page 116) or a slice of Torta di Nocciole (page 124). In the summer, it's often presented with fresh fruit and whipped cream or as the main ingredient in a frozen dessert.

In the top of a double boiler, beat the yolks and sugar for 3 minutes, or until they are creamy. Mix in the Moscato.

In the bottom of a double boiler, bring a few inches of water to a low simmer. Set the top of the double boiler over the water, making sure the bottom doesn't touch the water. Whisk the egg mixture continuously until it starts to become thick and fluffy—about 5 minutes.

Serve immediately in small cups or as a sauce with another dessert.

Monte Bianco

Chestnut Puree with Whipped Cream

6 SERVINGS

2 pounds fresh chestnuts,
in their shells

¼ teaspoon fennel seeds

1 bay leaf

1 cups milk

¼ cup sugar

2 ½ ounces hard amaretti cookies,
crushed (about 1 ¼ cups)

3 tablespoons unsweetened cocoa

2 tablespoons rum or cognac

1 ½ cups heavy cream

⅛ teaspoon vanilla extract

You may find this dessert in France under the name mont blanc, but it isn't clear whether the French or the Piedmontese created it first. It is easy to prepare and impressive to serve. Maria's mother, like many other Piemonte natives, made this winter dessert for the Christmas holidays.

Cut a slit in the shell of each chestnut. Place the chestnuts in a large pot with the fennel seeds and bay leaf, and cover with water. Bring the water to a boil and cook for 40 minutes.

Drain and discard the fennel seeds and bay leaf. Peel the chestnuts while warm and return them to the pot. Add the milk and cook for another 15 minutes, then mash the chestnuts with a fork and mix in the sugar. After another 15 minutes, pour the chestnuts into a bowl, and add the amaretti crumbs, cocoa, and rum. Let cool to room temperature.

Puree the chestnut mixture with a food mill onto a platter. The mixture will form a mound; don't pat it down.

Whip the cream with the vanilla extract until soft peaks form. Coat the chestnut puree with the whipped cream, using a spatula to form a mountain shape. Let it rest in the refrigerator for at least 2 hours and serve cold.

d

Pere Cotte in Vino Bianco
Pears Cooked in White Wine

This simple cooked fruit dessert is the perfect end to a multicourse Piedmontese meal. There, the Martin Sec pear is the most common variety; here, the Seckel pear provides a smaller but similarly flavored substitute.

4 SERVINGS

1 cup plus 2 tablespoons sugar

2 cups dry white wine

3 whole cloves

2 cinnamon sticks

2 pounds Seckel pears (about 8)

Combine 1 cup of the sugar, the wine, cloves, and cinnamon sticks in a nonreactive pan over low heat and stir until the sugar dissolves. Add the pears and simmer, covered, until they're fork tender, about 40 minutes. Remove from the pan and put into individual serving dishes. Raise the heat to medium and reduce the remaining liquid to a thick syrup, about 15 minutes more. Pour the warm syrup over the pears, sprinkle with the remaining 2 tablespoons sugar, and serve warm.

Zucchero Caramellato
Caramelized Sugar

Nothing exemplifies the Piedmontese use of simple ingredients like caramelized sugar. Just white sugar and a few drops of water are all there is to it, yet, it can bring a dessert to life and makes the difference between something plain and a wonderful dessert.

MAKES ⅓ CUP

¼ cup white sugar

Set a saucepan over a very low flame and pour in the sugar. Constantly tilt the saucepan over the heat until the sugar melts and begins to turn golden. Add a tablespoon of warm water a few drops at a time. (Be careful here! The sugar may spatter dangerously if you add the water too fast.) It's ready when the sugar is liquid and light brown, and the water is completely incorporated.

If you cook a dessert in a large metal mold, you can caramelize the sugar directly in it. However, if you plan to use ramekins, fill them with hot water to heat them—this will make it easier to distribute the caramelized sugar.

A Cup of Coffee

In Piemonte, just like the rest of Italy, you are never far from a cup of coffee. Not a big mug of Joe, but a "shot" whose concentration and flavor can vary enormously depending on how it's made and who makes it. Bars and restaurants have large espresso machines that use steam pressure to extract a very distinct flavor from the coffee beans, but, at home, the stovetop moka pot rules.

Coffee made in a moka isn't an inferior form of espresso, it's a whole different animal; a bit lighter and often much more complex. Unlike fancy espresso machines, moka pots can be purchased inexpensively and pressed into use without any preparation.

Making coffee this way is simple. First, fill the bottom reservoir with water. There should be just enough to touch the little valve on the side. Next put in the basket and fill it with ground coffee, just enough to reach the top rim. There's no need to tamp it down as you would in an espresso machine. Screw on the top and put the pot on a burner over medium heat. A few moments later, you'll hear the bubbling and gurgling that means your coffee is ready. Take it off the heat and serve.

We urge you to keep one or two moka pots in your kitchen and use them regularly. They make a wonderful change from filter coffee and are much easier to use than firing up a big espresso machine.

Vini Piemontesi

In Piemonte, like the rest of Italy, wine is part of everyday life. It's used in cooking and drunk at the table as an accompaniment to the food. Piemonte's wines, especially its reds, are recognized as among the best in Italy. Italian wines are identified by the geographical name of the district where the grapes grow. Thus the same grape variety can be used to make wines that are sold under different names. This system of naming wines recognizes that the terrain and the microclimate of an area are responsible for many of a wine's characteristics.

The best Piedmontese wines use Nebbiolo grapes. This name comes from the fog (nebbie) that envelops the vineyards in the early fall when Nebbiolo grapes are harvested. The best varieties of wine made with Nebbiolo are from the districts of Barolo (in Cuneo), Barbaresco (also in Cuneo), Carema (in Torino), and Gattinara (in Novara). These are full-bodied wines and need to age for few years to reach their peak.

Nebbiolos are complex, "important" wines that, in Piemonte, are not drunk with everyday meals. Most of the time, a good bottle of Dolcetto or Barbera is likely to be the choice. The sweet (*dolce*) Dolcetto grapes make a wine that is often compared with Beaujolais, from southern France. Like Beaujolais, Dolcetto is consumed young, generally between one and three years following its release. Dolcetto di Dogliani and Dolcetto d'Alba, both from the Langhe area, are the best examples.

Barbera is the most common wine grape in Piemonte and grows throughout the region. Every farmer used to grow Barbera grapes in its vineyards and make his own, all-too-often low-quality, wine. Big producers flooded the market with harsh Barbera as well, and all this damaged its reputation.

Wine[2]	Area	Grape	Best at
Barolo DOCG	Barolo (Cuneo)	Nebbiolo	5-10 years
Barbaresco DOCG	Barbaresco (Cuneo)	Nebbiolo	4-8 years
Carema DOC	Carema (Torino)	Nebbiolo	4-5 years
Gattinara DOC, DOCG	Vercelli	Nebbiolo	4 years
Ghemme DOC	Ghemme (Novara)	Nebbiolo	4 years
Nebbiolo d' Alba DOC	Alba (Cuneo)	Nebbiolo	2 years
Dolcetto di Dogliani DOC Dolcetto d' Alba DOC	Dogliani (Langhe) Alba (Langhe)	Dolcetto	1-3 years
Barbera d' Asti DOC Barbera d' Alba DOC	Asti Alba (Cuneo)	Barbera	1-2 years
Grignolino d' Asti DOC	Asti	Grignolino	12-18 months
Roero Arneis DOC	Roero (Cuneo)	Arneis	8-10 months
Asti Spumante Moscato d'Asti DOGC	Asti	White Moscato	6-8 months

2-DOC (**Denominazione di Origine Controllata**) *status are given to wines produced in limited area*
garantita e controllata) *a wine needs to be a DOC wine of a superior quality. DOGC wines und*

Description	Serving Suggestions
Full-bodied, garnet red wine with intense bouquet Alcohol level: 13-14%	Temperature: 68–71°F Best with: venison, wild birds, red meats, aged cheeses
Full-bodied, garnet red wine with intense bouquet Alcohol level: 12.5-13%	Temperature: 68°F Best with: meat roasts, grilled red meats, wild birds, aged cheeses
Full-bodied, garnet red wine with intense bouquet Alcohol level: 12.5-13%	Temperature: 68°F Best with: lamb, goat, grilled meats, mushrooms, goose, squab
Full-bodied, garnet red wine with intense bouquet Alcohol level: 12-13%	Temperature: 68°F Best with: meat roasts, venison, hare, hard cheeses
Full-bodied, garnet red wine with intense bouquet Alcohol level: 12-12.5%	Temperature: 68°F Best with: duck, red meats, snails, venison, hard cheeses
Full-bodied red wine Alcohol level: 12-12.5%	Temperature: 68°F Best with: meats, wild birds
Dry red wine with ruby and violet color Alcohol level: 11.5%	Temperature: 61–64°F Best with: chicken, rabbit, medium aged cheeses, salami
Full-bodied red wine Alcohol level: 12.5-13%	Temperature: 61°F Best with: agnolotti, bollito misto, oxtail, cotechino, red meats, salami
Light red wine with rubin red color Alcohol level: 11.5-12%	Temperature: 59–61degrees Best with: appetizers with delicate flavors, dry pasta dishes
White wine, yellow hay color Alcohol level: 12%	Temperature: 46–47°F Best with: omelets, vegetable soups, salt cod, fish
Sweet with yellow hay color, darker in Moscato and lighter in Spumante Alcohol level; 7%–8%	Temperature: 43–46°F Best with: sweet cakes and pastries, fruit salad

*g a controlled winemaking techniques. To be recognized as a DOGC (**Denominazione di origine** ter inspection that DOC wines.*

However, since the 1980s there has been a resurgence of Barbera, thanks to passionate growers who have planted the grapes in some of their better plots. Using these higher-quality grapes and applying sophisticated winemaking techniques, these producers were able to smooth its harshness and make Barbera respectable. Asti and Alba are the best known areas where Barbera is produced.

Piemonte is not a land of white wines, but Asti Spumante and Moscato, both made with the sweet Muscat grape are the best known. Asti Spumante is a fizzy wine and is bottled to look like champagne. Moscato has fewer and weaker bubbles, and is bottled in a regular wine bottle. Both are dessert wines that marry perfectly with chocolate and Piedmontese desserts.

Idee per Menu

[MENU IDEAS]

Spring

Cipolline in Agro Dolce (Sweet-and-Sour Onions)
Frittatine di erbe (Thin Herbed Omelets)
Insalata Capricciosa (Chicken and Ham Salad)

PRIMO

Tajarin con Sugo Burro e Salvia
(Egg Pasta with Butter and Sage)

SECONDO

Arrosto di Vitello (Veal Roast)
Spinaci al Burro (Sautéed Spinach)

DOLCE

Budino delle Langhe (Panna Cotta)

Summer

ANTIPASTI

Prosciutto in Gelatina (Ham Rolls in Aspic)
Caponet (Stuffed Zucchini Blossoms)
Sformato di Peperone con Salsa Rossa Estiva
(Bell Pepper Flan with Summer Red Sauce)

PRIMO

Gnocchetti di Ricotta con Funghi Trifolati
(Ricotta Gnocchi with Mushrooms)

SECONDO

Trota al Burro con Insalata Verde
(Sautéed Trout with a green salad)

DOLCE

Gianduiotto (Chocolate Almond Icebox Cake)

Autumn

Acciughe al Verde (Anchovies in Green Sauce)
Insalata di Carne Cruda (Raw Meat Salad)
Sformato di Spinaci con Fonduta (Spinach Flan with Cheese Sauce)

PRIMO

Risotto con Zucca (Risotto with Pumpkin)

SECONDO

Brasato al Vino Rosso con Carote Fritte
(Beef Cooked in Red Wine with Fried Carrots)

DOLCE

Bonet (Baked Chocolate Flan)

Winter

ANTIPASTI

Insalata Russa (Potato and Tuna Salad)
Cipolle Ripiene (Stuffed Onions)

PIATTO UNICO

Polenta con Coniglio al Civet (Polenta with Civet of Rabbit)
Polenta con Burro e Formaggi (Polenta with Butter and Cheese)

DOLCE

Pere Cotte in Vino Bianco (Pears Cooked in White Wine)

Bibliografia

[BIBLIOGRAPHY]

Doglio, Sandro. *L'Inventore della Bagna Cauda*. Cuneo: Edizioni Daumerie, 1993.

Gambera, Armando, ed. *Ricette delle Osterie di Langa*. Bra: Arcigola Slow Food, 1992.

Goria, Giovanni. *La Cucina del Piemonte*. Padua: Franco Muzzio & Company, 1990.

Kramer, Matt. *A Passion For Piedmont: Italy's Most Glorious Regional Table*. New York: William Morrow & Company Inc., 1997.

Schena, Elma and Adriano Ravera. *La Cucina di Madonna Lesina*. Cuneo: Edizioni L'Arciere, 1988.

Schena, Elma and Adriano Ravera. *Le Galuppiere del Vecchio Piemonte*. Cuneo: Edizioni, L'Arciere, 1991.

Indice

[INDEX]

From Hippocrene's Italian Library

CUISINE

SICILIAN FEASTS
Giovanna Bellia La Marca
Sicilian Feasts was born out of the author's love for her native Sicily. She shares the history, customs, and folklore, as well as the flavorful and varied cuisine of her beautiful Mediterranean island in recipes, stories, and anecdotes. Sicilian Feasts offers more than 160 recipes, along with menus for holidays, notes on ingredients, list of suppliers, an introduction to the Sicilian language, and a glossary of food terms in Sicilian, Italian, and English. Illustrations demonstrate special techniques.
220 pages • 6 x 9 • two-color • 0-7818-0967-3 • $24.95hc • (539)

CUCINA DI CALABRIA: TREASURED RECIPES
AND FAMILY TRADITIONS FROM SOUTHERN ITALY
Mary Amabile Palmer
Mary Amabile Palmer has gathered a comprehensive collection of exciting, robust recipes from the home of her ancestors. **Cucina di Calabria** is a celebration of the cuisine she knows intimately and loves, a cuisine as adventurous and creative as any in Italy. This volume includes nearly 200 recipes with something for every cook, whether novice or experienced. All make use of fresh, simple ingredients that are transformed into sumptuous dishes with minimum effort. They are interwoven with anecdotes about Calabrian culture and history, traditions, and folklore.
320 pages • 8 x 10 • 0-7818-1050-7 • $18.95hc • (660)

A TREASURY OF ITALIAN CUISINE (BILINGUAL)
RECIPES, SAYINGS AND PROVERBS IN ITALIAN AND ENGLISH
Learn the basics of hearty and delicious Italian cooking in this appealing bilingual cookbook. Among the 60 recipes in Italian and English are such staples as Cozze alla Parmigiana (Baked Mussels), Minestrone, Salsa di Pomodoro (Basic Tomato Sauce), Ossobuco al Marsala (Veal Shanks in Marsala), and Cannoli Siciliani (Sicilian Cannoli), all adapted for the modern cook and the North American kitchen. Line drawings, proverbs and bits of folk wisdom add to the volume's charm. This book is the perfect gift for students of the Italian culinary tradition, culture and language.
146 pages • 5 x 7 • line drawings • 0-7818-0740-9 • $11.95hc • (149)

LANGUAGE GUIDES

INSTANT ITALIAN VOCABULARY BUILDER
Tom Means
Instantly add thousands of words to your Italian using word-ending patterns! Many words in French and Italian are nearly the same as their English counterparts due to

their common Latin origin. The only difference is the word ending. For example, you can translate most English words ending in –ous into Italian by changing the ending to –oso ("misteri–oso"). Because each of these patterns applies to hundreds of words, by learning them you can increase your vocabulary instantly.

CD • 4,000 entries • 224 pages • 6 x 9 • 0-7818-0980-0 • $14.95pb • (476)

BEGINNER'S ITALIAN
Joseph F. Privitera

A delightful and instructive invitation to Italy! This introductory guide teaches the structure of the Italian language, covering essential grammar in twelve lessons, along with practice dialogues, vocabulary and expressions, and review exercises. An introduction to the Italian culture, including geography, history, economy, and arts and letters, as well as practical advice for the traveler, completes this self-study course.

192 pages • 5 ½ x 8 ½ • 0-7818-0839-1 • $14.95pb • (208)

ITALIAN-ENGLISH/ENGLISH-ITALIAN CONCISE DICTIONARY
Federica K. Clementi

Italian, spoken by nearly 60 million people worldwide, remains one of the most popular languages among students today. This essential reference contains more than 16,000 keywords and includes examples to help clarify ambiguous meanings. Basic vocabulary words, technological terms, and idiomatic expressions are also provided. The pronunciation section demonstrates the cardinal rules of the spoken language, while the compact grammar section examines sentence structure, part of speech, and syntax, among other aspects. An appendix of important verbs completes this dictionary, which comprises an invaluable tool for travelers, students, and diplomats alike.

16,000 entries • 400 pages • 4 x 6 • 0-7818-1046-9 • $14.95pb • (631)

ITALIAN-ENGLISH/ENGLISH-ITALIAN PRACTICAL DICTIONARY
35,000 entries • 433 pages • 5 ½ x 8 ½ • 0-7818-0354-3 • $12.95pb • (201)

HIPPOCRENE CHILDREN'S ILLUSTRATED ITALIAN DICTIONARY
English-Italian/Italian-English
• for ages 5 and up
• 500 entries with color pictures
• commonsense pronunciation for each Italian word
• Italian-English index

500 entries • 94 pages • 8 ½ x 11 • 0-7818-0771-9 • $14.95hc • (355)

MASTERING ADVANCED ITALIAN
278 pages • 5 1/2 x 8 1/2 • 0-7818-0333-0 • $14.95pb • (160)
2 cassettes: 0-7818-0334-9 • $12.95 • (161)

ITALIAN-ENGLISH/ENGLISH-ITALIAN DICTIONARY & PHRASEBOOK
Federica K. Clementi

This concise language guide includes a bilingual dictionary and a phrasebook with use-

ful topics such as greetings, travel and transportation, accommodations, dining out, health, and more. Cultural information and a basic Italian grammar complement the vocabulary and phrases. It is ideal for students or those traveling to Italy.
2,500 entries • 216 pages • 3 ¾ x 7 ½ • 0-7818-0812-X • $11.95pb • (137)

SICILIAN-ENGLISH/ENGLISH-SICILIAN DICTIONARY & PHRASEBOOK
Joseph F. Privitera
The speech of the Sicilian people bears the imprint of the island's remarkable history. Primarily based on Latin and Italian, it contains traces of Greek, Arabic, French, Old Provençal, and Spanish.

This book features a concise Sicilian grammar and a bilingual dictionary with pronunciation guide. The comprehensive phrasebook offers guidance for situations including dining out, accommodations, and obtaining medical care. It also contains complete phonetic spellings.
3,600 entries • 200 pages • 3 ¾ x 7 ½ • 0-7818-0984-3 • $11.95pb• (494)

BEGINNER'S SICILIAN
Joseph F. Privitera
This introductory guide teaches the structure of the Sicilian language, covering essential grammar in 10 lessons, along with practice dialogues, vocabulary and expressions, and review exercises. An introduction to the Sicilian culture, including geography, history, economy, and arts and letters, as well as practical information for the traveler complete this course of study.
159 pages • 5 ½ x 8 ½ • 0-7818-0640-2 • $11.95pb • (716)

HISTORY AND CULTURE

ITALY: AN ILLUSTRATED HISTORY
Joseph F. Privitera
This concise, illustrated volume covers the full panoply of Italy's history—from Roman times to the twenty-first century, including accounts of major political and social events that shaped the country. Focusing on artistic and cultural accomplishments and the figures behind them, Dante, Verdi, among many others, the work offers background and insight into this fascinating culture.
140 pages • 50 b/w photos/illus./maps • 5 x 7 • 0-7818-0819-7 • $14.95hc • (436)

SICILY: AN ILLUSTRATED HISTORY
Joseph F. Privitera
This history relates how Sicily became one of the first centers of civilization of greater Italy, home to many of the world's most distinguished philosophers, mathematicians, scientists, and artists. The narrative subsequently recounts the region's millennium-long decline at the hands of foreign invaders, its hard-won battle for freedom in 1860 under the leadership of Giuseppe Garibaldi, and its current status as a center of art and tourism.
152 pages • 5 x 7 • 50 b/w photos/illus./maps • 0-7818-0909-6 • $12.95pb • (301)

LITERATURE

TREASURY OF ITALIAN LOVE POEMS, QUOTATIONS & PROVERBS
Joseph F. Privitera
Spanning Italy's rich romantic tradition, this collection includes 26 poems and over 100 quotations and proverbs. Featured are poems from such famous figures as Dante Alighieri, Francesco Petrarcho, Lorenzo de'Medici, and Michelangelo Buanarroti. Each selection appears in Italian with side by side English translation. Also available as an audiobook.
128 pages • 5 x 7 • 0-7818-0352-7 • W •$11.95hc • (587)
Cassettes: 0-7818-0366-7 • $12.95 • (581)

DICTIONARY OF 1,000 ITALIAN PROVERBS
Organized alphabetically by key words, this bilingual reference book is a guide to and information source for a key element of Italian.
131 pages • 5 ½ x 8 ½ • 0-7818-0458-2 • W • $11.95pb • (370)

Prices subject to change without prior notice. To purchase Hippocrene Books contact your local bookstore, visit www.hippocrenebooks.com, call (718) 454-2366, or write to: HIPPOCRENE BOOKS, 171 Madison Avenue, New York, NY 10016. Please enclose check or money order, adding $5.00 shipping (UPS) for the first book, and $.50 for each additional book.